REFL**E**CTIONS

OF AN ENTREPRENEUR

The Story of
FISH Window Cleaning

MIKE MERRICK
with Linda Merrick

REFLECTIONS OF AN ENTREPRENEUR
The Story of Fish Window Cleaning
Mike Merrick with Linda Merrick

Published by Ripples Publishing Company, Ellisville, MO

The product information and advice provided (in this book) are intended for general informational purposes only. The author and publisher of this book have made every effort to ensure that the content is accurate and up-to-date at the time of publication. However, they make no representations or warranties of any kind, express or implied, about the completeness, accuracy, reliability, suitability, or availability of the information, products, or services contained in this book for any purpose.

Project Management and Book Design: Davis Creative, LLC,
    dba: DavisCreativePublishing.com
Cover Design: Missy Asikainen
Editor: Pam Wilson
Copyeditor: Kim Fletcher

Publisher's Cataloging-in-Publication
Names: Merrick, Mike, 1947- author. | Merrick, Linda, 1948- author.
Title: Reflections of an entrepreneur : the story of Fish Window Cleaning /
    Mike Merrick, with Linda Merrick.
Description: Ellisville, MO : Ripples Publishing Company, [2025] |
    Includes bibliographical references.
Identifiers: LCCN: 2025900969 | ISBN: 9798992441901 (hardcover) |
    9798992441925 (paperback) | 9798992441918 (ebook)
Subjects: LCSH: Merrick, Mike, 1947- | Fish Window Cleaning (Firm) |
    Businesspeople--United States--Biography. | Entrepreneurship--
    Anecdotes. | Success in business--Anecdotes. | LCGFT: Autobiographies.
    | Anecdotes. | BISAC: BIOGRAPHY & AUTOBIOGRAPHY / Business.
    | BUSINESS & ECONOMICS / Entrepreneurship. | BUSINESS &
    ECONOMICS / General.
Classification: LCC: HC102.5.M462 A3 2025 | DDC: 338.092--dc23

ENDORSEMENTS

"Mike and Linda Merrick are two of the best business owners I know. Mike and Linda are both gifted leaders and created a Fish Window Cleaning vision that gets results. As goes the leaders, so goes the team. When I met Mike once a week, we reviewed the sales numbers. Mike believes in accountability and in sales. Results are everything, and they do not lie! They love God and they love their people well."

Donnie Williams,
Salesforce One

"I first heard Mike and Linda's story in 2002 as I was investigating their franchise opportunities with Fish Window Cleaning. I loved what I heard then and knew I wanted to be part of their system. Their story has only gotten better since. I think you will love reading this book."

Randy Cross
Franchisee in Grand Rapids, Michigan

"I've known and worked closely with Mike and Linda Merrick for over twenty years. This association has been one of the best in my lifetime because they are very special people. Most folks in business care about making money and that's obviously their focus. Mike and Linda, though, also care about helping others. They always lead from the heart and assume that if they stay true to that focus, then the money will take care of itself. It's been an incredible honor for me to have the wonderful business relationship and personal friendship I have with great leaders like Mike and Linda. Big hugs to both!"

Jeff Elgin
Chief Executive Officer
FranChoice, Inc.

"The story of Mike and Linda's ascent to business success is a timeless inspiration for anyone, especially those starting a business. I have had the pleasure of knowing Mike and Linda both personally and professionally for many years. One night, Mike and Linda hosted a dinner for a small group. Mike asked if I'd like to join him in another room for a game of ping-pong. Little did I know he was using this game as an "interview" and probably character test. As we paddled back and forth, he asked questions about financial and estate planning. After he got what he wanted, he quickly changed from amateur Mike into Ping-Pong Champion USA. He walloped me in a matter of minutes and then said, "Thanks," and we walked back to the party. That was it. It was classic Mike. My favorite part about their story is how they practice what they preach, literally. The Merricks are some of the most generous folks I have ever met. Taking scriptural truths and putting them into action to encourage and bless those around them. It's a joy to watch and an inspiration to everyone around."

Brett A. Goldschmidt
Certified Financial Planner

Merrick family pictured left to right:
Sam, Matt, Tammy, Eve, Linda, Mike, Catherine, and Nate

DEDICATION

I am grateful for my wife, Linda, the love of my life. Without her, none of my crazy business ventures and adventures could have materialized.

Matt and Nathan have been involved in work and play since the beginning. Matt is not shy about expressing his strong opinions, and Nathan has ideas that one can almost see oozing out of his pores. Thank you for who you are.

Thank you to my daughters-in-law who are really my daughters. Tammy and Catherine, you have been pillars of support to our sons and our family business.

To my grandchildren, Sam and Eve. Thank you for opening my imagination in so many ways. You have been my guides into a wondrous land. The narrator of an old television show, *The Twilight Zone*, described it this way: "You're traveling through another dimension, a dimension not only of sight and sound but of mind. A journey into a wondrous land whose boundaries are that of imagination."

I have written this book to honor the Lord and express publicly the many ways He has touched my life. He answered my prayers in unexpected ways, and the story of Fish Window Cleaning is just one.

This is a promise from Psalms that is still being fulfilled:

"He brought me forth also into a large place." Psalm 18:19

TABLE OF CONTENTS

NATHAN'S FOREWORD

My dad compliments me that I am a fast window cleaner. He sent me out on window cleaning routes before I was old enough to drive with one of his cleaners, who was passionate about efficiency. This employee knew that time was money. On each job, he showed me where to place my bucket so I wouldn't have to move it as often, when and only when to use the extension pole. He highlighted the customer service experience by doing a slight touchup on the door after someone signed the work order to show the customer we cared about our work. My window cleaning experience prepared me to support new franchisees as they hired window cleaners.

My primary job, starting with FISH, was to provide onsite support for grand openings and ongoing support trips, the purpose of which was to drive sales through cold-calling. Later, our executive team worked with a consultant who encouraged me to focus my time on franchise development, rather than operations. I found my lane working in sales and leading the sales team, helping prospective franchisees in their investigation, and due diligence to join FISH.

People always ask, "Who would buy a window cleaning franchise?" Our franchisees include engineers, doctors, lawyers, fighter pilots, chefs, veterans, marketing executives, IT executives, teachers, and Wall Street brokers. We have female owners, veterans, minorities, and individuals who have relocated from across the United States or overseas to open the franchise. More recently, we've seen younger people choosing to bypass corporate America altogether and take the leap directly into business ownership. However, the largest demographic of FISH franchise owners is men and women with vast experience in corporate America who are seeking a bold career change, an improvement in work-life balance, and the chance to build equity in something sustainable. In my experience, our franchisees are passionate about their cities and the opportunities to build their businesses in their communities.

I tell many people that I was fortunate to get in on the ground floor of FISH, which is technically accurate since FISH is still growing all these years later, but I came into the business full-time in year three. I cannot overstate the long hours my dad, mom, and Matt put into the company before I arrived, for which I am eternally grateful. I watched my parents set the bar high for working together, and now our work family has expanded as my wife, Catherine, and Matt's wife, Tammy, are full-time board members. As I write this afternoon, Matt and Tammy are traveling and working on a FISH property, while Catherine is mocking up designs for our office's new entryway. I hope you enjoy reading this book and the inspiring stories leading up to FISH and its franchising. Matt and I are incredibly fortunate to have grown up with entrepreneurial parents. I even learned many details I didn't know about my parents in the pages ahead.

MATT'S FOREWORD

My mom and dad started Fish Window Cleaning when I was three-and-a-half years old. They already owned Wheel House Manor Mobile Home Court by that time, so I grew up in an entrepreneurial household. I did not understand how special it was at the time, but I never heard my parents say, "Sorry, I won't be home for dinner because I have to work late." Or, "I have to go out of town on a business trip." My parents were always present and involved in our lives. Not only did we grow up with both parents, but we had the added blessing of growing up with two sets of grandparents who loved us in ways only grandparents know how. I am saddened as an adult when I meet and hear the stories from friends about the heartaches they experienced from their broken families. I am more grateful every day for my family relationships, including my wife, Tammy, and our children, Sam and Eve.

A household supported by more than one small family business means the children are "employees," whether they know it or not. On many Saturday mornings my dad would come through saying, "It's time to rock 'n' roll!" I knew what that meant. It was time to go dig a hole at Wheel House Manor or push a wheelbarrow full of concrete. Sometimes, it meant digging a hole just to fill it with concrete a few minutes later. You have not lived until, with only a shovel and the faith in what seems impossible, you dig through something that, in no way, resembles soil. Jefferson County, Missouri, is known for its rocky ground with compact clay. When a sewer line that led to a mobile home collapsed, we were the work crew responsible to fix it. Not all forty-two mobile home sewer lines collapsed at the same time, but this was one of many ongoing maintenance projects that needed attention. On days when we didn't have to dig a hole or pour concrete, we got what was considered the light work of sweeping the street, all 976 feet of it, including the cul-de-sac, by hand, with a push broom. To this day, I don't know why, but it seemed like that street always needed sweeping.

As I got a little older, if I was off school, then I got to clean windows. I was around ten years old when I went on my first window-cleaning job at a KFC restaurant. It was my job to mop the windows, while my dad followed behind and squeegeed the windows and towel dried the sills. Mopping was the easiest part, but I was still learning and wasn't fast enough. Dad would always catch up to me. I think this was my first and second business lesson all rolled into one, and both have stuck with me:

1. There is a big difference between activity and productivity.

2. Time is money.

The window cleaning business is built on these two principles, and I'm glad I learned them at an early age.

These work experiences were great, and I remember most of them fondly. My childhood was comprised of many wonderful experiences. Sometimes I played soccer, baseball, or rode my bike. Our family loved camping, water skiing, and building sandcastles on the beach. When I was nine years old, we took a 7,000-mile trip touring the west in an RV. The trip included visits to many national parks and concluded with roasting marshmallows around a campfire each night. Whether it was sports, a simple hike in the woods, or spending the night with our grandparents, there was a lot of free time to be a kid. But, when I heard my dad's voice and call to action, I knew it was time to rock 'n' roll.

A MESSAGE FROM LINDA MERRICK

I want to introduce you to my husband, friend, and business partner, Mike Merrick. Mike and I met at our church youth group while we were in high school. We attended different high schools, so we got acquainted at this central meeting place from our homes. Church was more than just a building to hang out. It was a special place where we met and formed relationships with each other and several people who became life-long friends. Since meeting, falling in love, and getting married, we have walked on a foundation of common faith, trust in our God, and a commitment to each other. Many commitments are unspoken, but early on, Mike and I verbalized we would not threaten each other with the "D" word, "divorce," and in tough times we would not run.

We had time to mature and grow and enjoy our relationship as a couple before we welcomed our first son Matthew, who arrived in June 1974. We brought him home from the hospital on our seventh wedding anniversary and Father's Day. Two years later, our second son, Nathan, completed our family.

I had an inkling of how busy life would be with two energetic boys, but I had no idea what adventures were in store for me while sharing the dreams of a budding entrepreneur. Couples usually anticipate there will be hills and valleys with a few mountaintops throughout their lives. However, the road traveled with an entrepreneur is more like leaping across chasms and diving off cliffs. In the movie, *Butch Cassidy and the Sundance Kid*, Butch says to Sundance, "I have vision; the rest of the world is wearing bifocals."

Vision, hope, and faith are our trifecta after fifty-seven years.

INTRODUCTION

My wife, Linda, and I survived raising two teenage sons. I say that mostly tongue-in-cheek because as I reflect on it twenty-five years later, it could have been worse. I encountered various situations as a parent that brought out anger and frustration. Now I can laugh at the head-butting that ensued when each son pushed my "Who's boss here?" button. Anyone who has tried to have a serious conversation with a fourteen-year-old boy understands what I mean when I say, "Deer in the headlights look." Thankfully, today, I enjoy wonderful relationships with our adult sons, Matt and Nathan, and their spouses, Tammy and Catherine. There is not enough space for me to tell you about my two grandchildren, Sam and Eve. They are the best with a capital B. If you have grandchildren, I'm sure they are the best, too.

I used to tell people I was self-employed. Most people do not understand what that means. I am quite sure they think, "Does he have a real job?" My mother did not understand self-employment either. I did not work for a company in the same way my father and brother did. They retired from Chevrolet and Ford, respectively. Mom could tell her friends where her husband and oldest son worked. People recognized Chevy and Ford as legitimate workplaces. On the other hand, she would call me in the middle of the day and say, "Your brother is working, and I need you to take me to my doctor's appointment." Early on, I would try to say something like, "I am at work too," but eventually, it became easier to rearrange my schedule and take her to her appointment. Accommodating her perpetuated the myth that I did not have a real job. Remember, this was before cottage industries and side hustles burst on the scene and definitely before working from home changed the business landscape.

As my start-up business endeavors began to grow and became more successful, I serendipitously gave myself a promotion and a new title: business owner. I felt good about that title. My wife started telling people I was an entrepreneur; they tried not to laugh. A few of my friends were corporate executives who saw themselves as chiefs sitting around the campfire while I fetched wood. Bruce, whom I met at church, was the exception. He came from a poor family in eastern Kentucky but went to college and accepted an entry-level position with a large retail pharmaceutical company. He worked hard and was eventually promoted to senior vice president. I cannot fully explain why, but Bruce and I connected. He respected what I did and understood that even though my financials were peanuts compared to the mammoth corporation he worked for, success still came down to one question: How do you beat the competition at their game?

Recently, I gave myself another title: Founder. I founded one of my corporations in 1978, and today, we have 275 locations in forty-five states. Maybe you have heard of us – Fish Window Cleaning. We provide professional commercial and residential window cleaning. Our brand colors are red and white. Our vans and vehicles are bright red with a white logo. Customers and acquaintances tell me, "I saw your red van." We like to call them our rolling billboards. We have red logo apparel and hats, and I wear my red shirt and hat everywhere I go. It makes for easy packing when going on vacation: red shirt, hat, and khaki shorts or pants. While on an idyllic Baltic Cruise, I was enjoying a small group tour in St. Petersburg, Russia, when a woman said to me, "Your company cleans my windows in West Chester, New York." I said, "Yes, that is Mike S. He does an excellent job." I have learned to keep it short and sweet.

I do not stress about my title or try to explain to someone how I got the idea to start franchising. You will read more about that as my story unfolds. For the most part, it is easier to tell someone I meet that I am a window cleaner because most people do not understand franchising. A person may know the term "franchise" because of restaurants like McDonald's or even sports teams. When I worked full-time and people asked me what I did for a living, I answered, "I franchise a window cleaning business." There it was: the deer-in-the-headlights look. I would suddenly have flashbacks of trying to talk with one of my fourteen-year-old sons. One day, I spoke to a fellow at church who seemed interested in a more in-depth talk about my business and learning about our expansion. I tried to explain window-cleaning franchises to him. After a few minutes, he said, "Now, let me get this straight. Mike, you expect people to pay you to teach them how to clean windows?" I finally said, "Well, it is *something* like that."

I started Fish Window Cleaning in 1978, and we opened our first franchise location in 1998. After forty-seven years, I jokingly say, "I am an overnight success." In 2014, I took a step back. We formed a family Board of Directors, composed of our sons, their wives, and Linda and me. We hired one of our franchisees – Randy Cross from Grand Rapids, Michigan – as our President of Fish Window Cleaning, Services, Inc., our franchise sales, and training corporation. I still go to the office at least one day a week. At our board meetings, we discuss big-picture issues, and Randy and our staff of twenty-six awesome employees manage the day-to-day operations.

You would think at this stage of life, my deer-in-the-headlights stories would be less frequent, but not really. In the past, people wanted to know who I worked for, especially insurance or finance people I met when I tried to get a car loan. They did not think they could trust me to pay my bills since I was self-employed. Now, I find myself in a different dilemma: Am I still working, or am I retired? Somehow, we all are supposed to fit into a neat category. At least Medicare wants me to fit into a category.

I should have learned my lesson: It did not work when I tried to explain franchising to someone who only wanted to know if I was employed. However, I am a slow learner. One day, I stood at the hospital check-in counter waiting for a simple procedure. The desk person asked me, "Are you retired?" I responded, "I own a business, but I am not working full time." I was trying to be helpful, I really was, but the desk person had to ask again, "Are you working or retired?" Cue the deer-in-the-headlights look. I guess an "either-or" box was my only option. So, I made the grievous mistake of answering, "I am still working." Based on my response, the desk person handed me another sheet of paper in addition to the five sheets I already had to complete. Then, Medicare wanted to know if my employer was my primary insurer. I pity the people who had to endure me explaining that as the owner of the company, I receive dividends, but I am not on my company's insurance plan. Finally, I woke up. I am retired. If Medicare can live with that, so can I.

Fish Window Cleaning Services hosts an annual convention for our franchisees to attend educational sessions, round tables, and panel discussions. I love one of our segments, "30 Ideas in 30 Minutes." We strive to have valuable content at this three-day event and encourage attendees to go home with three golden nuggets that will help them improve their local franchises. What are golden nuggets? They are business ideas that require franchisees to dig deep to grasp how these concepts can positively influence the way they run their day-to-day operations. It is not easy to let go of habits that do not produce the results we want. These habits may not always be wrong, but there may be a more productive way to accomplish the end result.

I have not written a "how to run a business" book. Business concepts are interspersed throughout, and spiritual inspiration is sprinkled on top. You may only want to skim the surface and move on. Regardless, my sincere hope is that you will find at least three nuggets that may take a little work to dig and uncover, but you will deem valuable to apply in your life and business pursuits.

CHAPTER 1:

Linda's Story in Her Own Words

"Love is friendship that has caught fire."

–ANN LANDERS

I am grateful to have known two very special people from the "Greatest Generation," my parents, James Henry Prentice (Henry) and Edna Davis. I am a baby boomer. I embrace this title as more than just an adult who now receives Social Security benefits and discounts at fast food chains. As a prodigy of a World War II Navy veteran, I was welcomed by my parents who very much wanted a child in 1948. I recently saw a social media post on Memorial Day that read, "Remember the fallen veterans who did not come home and who did not have children to honor them today." When I look at the photo of my dad in his Navy dress blues that hangs on the wall in my office, I am thankful for the hand of Providence that spared his life and granted me life. I am thankful for my parents who loved me. I encourage children to ask their parents questions. There are things I don't know about my dad and mom that I wish I did. When it is too late to ask, it is too late.

My father was born in 1915 in the hills of Tennessee. His birth was at home, and he never had an official birth certificate, only a document from a census that was taken when he was four years old. He was the baby of eight children. His father abandoned the family when he was only eight years old. The older brothers had to become the "men" of the house. My dad didn't talk about the hardships of extreme poverty much. He did not dwell on it and told me it's not good to keep blaming other people for their mistakes. He told me his older brothers had to shoot rabbits and other small game for the family to eat. When he was fourteen years old, my father, Henry, made the decision to come to St. Louis, Missouri, to find a job in the big city. I am unable to imagine all the emotions he must have experienced when he arrived in a city with a bustling population of 800,000. I do not remember him telling me how he made this 400-mile trip from Silver Point, Tennessee, to St Louis. He got a job at a bar/restaurant in downtown St. Louis. This establishment was owned by a Greek immigrant. He gave my dad a room on the second floor of the bar to live in and hired him as a dishwasher. This was his first introduction to the food service industry. The year was 1929 and the beginning of the Great Depression.

My mother, Edna Davis, was born in 1919 and grew up on a farm in rural Missouri with her parents and ten siblings. From the stories she told me, they always had enough to eat because of a garden, chickens, and ingenuity. She worked in the fields picking cotton as a young girl and did not have her first pair of shoes until it was time to go to school. She left home and the farming community at seventeen to move to St. Louis to find a job. There were large homes in the Central West End of St. Louis, and the owners would occasionally rent upstairs rooms to young, single women. Mom lived in one room and worked various jobs, mostly as a waitress. She eventually became a Harvey Girl at the Fred Harvey Restaurant in downtown Union Station in the late 1930s. The *Harvey Girls* was a novel published in 1942 by Samuel Hopkins Adams. In 1946, it was adapted by MGM into a musical film of the same name, starring Judy Garland. The *Harvey Girls* epitomized grace and hospitality in the Fred Harvey Restaurants located primarily in railroad stations. Mom told me apple pie was the signature dessert, and some patrons would order a slice of cheddar cheese on top, which was an oddball request to a country girl like my mother. My dad got a job as a bartender at the Fred Harvey Restaurant in 1941, where my parents met. They had a few months to date before the bombing of Pearl Harbor on December 7, 1941, "a date that will live in infamy."

My dad knew he would be drafted into the Army, so he enlisted in the Navy. My parents were married in March 1942, with the world at war. After completing boot camp at the Naval Station Great Lakes in Chicago, Dad was stationed in San Diego. Mom took a train out west to live there while he waited to receive his orders. He shipped out of San Diego with the only orders the enlisted sailors were given, "Destination unknown."

The South Pacific and the chain of the New Hebrides Islands, specifically Espiritu Santo, became his home for the next two years. The few letters he was able to send home could not contain any information about where he was or what he was doing. Mom was like countless other women left at home to live under a cloud of uncertainty. While my dad was deployed, my mother returned to St. Louis to work again at the Fred Harvey's Restaurant in the St. Louis Union Station. I can't pretend to understand what it was like for the spouses and families who manned the home front during World War II. After Dad returned from serving in the Navy, he and Mom continued to work in St. Louis doing what they knew, the food service industry.

My mother had a childhood friend, Dorothy, who also worked at the Fred Harvey Restaurant during the war. Following World

War II, Dorothy and her husband decided to move to Arkansas to start a new carefree life after all the stresses of wartime. Somehow, they convinced my parents this would be a good idea for them too. As an adult, I teased my parents and joked with them about how I was glad they made this big mistake, so they could at least forgive me for one big mistake I might make at some point in my life. This move to Arkansas did not turn out to be the Utopia they envisioned. My dad built a concrete block house without indoor plumbing or running water. It was during this Arkansas adventure, I was almost born on the side of a dirt road while my parents raced in a pickup truck to the closest hospital in Morrilton, Arkansas. In November 1948, they welcomed me as their first-born. They had been married for six years and had experienced the interruption of war. My mother was twenty-nine years old and was very excited about having a daughter. They stayed in Arkansas less than a year before realizing they needed to move back to St. Louis to do what they knew best, run a restaurant.

My dad's brother, Pat, also lived in St. Louis after returning from serving in the Navy. Pat died unexpectedly from a carbon monoxide leak from a gas heater. His widow, Vesta, bought a two-family flat in South St. Louis. She wanted my dad to live close by because she knew she could depend on him. These flats were sometimes called shotgun houses because each floor had three rooms, a living room in front, bedroom in the middle, and kitchen in the rear. If a person stood at the front door, they could see all the way through to the back wall of the flat.

Aunt Vesta lived upstairs and Dad, Mom, and I lived downstairs. I loved this cozy arrangement. Aunt Vesta never had children of her own, and she was like a second mother to me. She took me shopping and to the movies. She let me drink coffee with copious amounts of milk and sugar. She convinced my mom to let me get my first pair of nylons and dressy black patent leather shoes. Aunt Vesta and I would walk hand in hand to the local library. She introduced me to children's classics such as *Heidi*, *The Little Lame Prince*, and *Little Women*. I have happy memories as a child of playing in the yard and skating with clip-on roller skates on the concrete sidewalk. I had more than my share of skinned-up knees as proof of my love of roller skating.

In February 1955, my sister, Donna, was born. I had been an only child for six years and Mom knew she needed to help prepare me for a sibling. She gave me the honor of naming my sister. Think about this. What god-awful names could a six-year-old imagine? Fortunately, I had a good friend in dance school, Donna Marie. I told Mom I wanted to name my baby sister, "Donna Marie." There it was, a beautiful name for a beautiful blond-headed baby girl. I had a few dolls, but now I had a real-life baby sissy. I had the privilege of feeding her bottled formula while having my own bottle of chocolate milk along with her. I pushed her around for hours in an adorable baby buggy on the sidewalk that encircled our two-family flat.

My dad bought a piece of land along the Meramec River in Fenton, Missouri. Dad had a natural talent for building things, and he began construction on what was to be our two-story, three-bedroom house. In August 1957, we moved in preparation for my enrollment in a new elementary school. I was excited about having my own bedroom and a stylish new bedroom set. I was sad at the same time, though, because Aunt Vesta would not be in close proximity. I was also nervous about trying to make friends. The road we lived on did not have sidewalks and the street was a combination of tar and gravel. This type of surface was not conducive to roller skating. All the neighborhood kids had bikes. I was desperate to learn how to ride a bicycle. My dad bought me a used bike that cost fourteen dollars. It took a while for me to get the hang of bike riding, but I loved it. The neighborhood "gang" would ride to the local swimming pool during the summer and be gone all day. We loved the independence riding our bikes gave us, and our parents did not worry about us because we were safe in the 1950s. Christmas Day of 1960 was a special day. Brand-spanking-new cobalt blue bikes were under the tree for both my sister and me.

I rode the bus to elementary school and eventually to high school. Several members of our 1966 class of Eureka High School formed close relations during these long bus rides and after-school activities. Many of us have stayed in touch and still get together to celebrate milestone graduation anniversaries, including ten, twenty-five, fifty, and fifty-five years.

My parents opened the Hi-Way House restaurant in Fenton, the same year we moved to the county in 1957. My parents worked long hours at the restaurant, and I was left at home to babysit my younger sister. I wish I could say I was a better older sister, but there was excessive bossing on my part that resulted in many arguments. My job, besides babysitting and cleaning the house, was to put the change my parents brought home from the restaurant into paper coin rolls to take to the bank with the daily deposits. I rolled hundreds of pennies, dimes, nickels, and quarters, week in and week out. This was my parents' way of teaching me how to help in the family business. I did not wait tables because they served alcohol, and I was too young. My sister was only two years old, and my primary job was to help watch her because of the long hours our parents worked.

I loved school and I was a good student. I earned top grades, and I liked participating in extracurricular activities like the National Honor Society, the Girls Athletic Association, marching band, and drama club.

When I was in high school, my mother started talking to me about becoming a nurse after graduation. I think she wished she would have had the opportunity to have an education and be a nurse. She had a very caring heart and helped family and friends. She especially helped my sister and me when we became adults and had our own children. Mom understood busy moms need relief from hectic schedules and need some quiet time for them-selves. Every Friday, our sons Matt and Nathan would go to the grandparents' house. Our boys loved it. They rode Big Wheels and occasionally had ice cream for breakfast. This gave Mike and me the opportunity to have a date night.

Grandparents get to have the fun of enjoying little ones in a way they didn't with their own children because of long work hours. We enjoyed having similar experiences with our grandchildren. The important life lesson I learned from Mom can be summed up in the word "sacrifice." She put the needs of her children before her own. This was not done by handing out lavish gifts or having a no-rules policy. It was just her way to help and be there for others with a humble spirit. She lived to be ninety-five years old, and she loved to iron to still feel useful.

When I was fourteen, I decided to volunteer during the summer as a candy striper. I know a candy striper does not do what a nurse does, but this experience helped me realize the nursing profession was not my calling. I visited a couple of four-year college campuses in Missouri to help me decide what I wanted to do when I graduated. My Aunt Vesta told me about Miss Hickey's

Business College in St. Louis. I decided I wanted to attend this business college after high school graduation. Aunt Vesta showed me what shorthand notes looked like. It seemed shorthand was similar to a foreign language. I took piano lessons for about ten years and had great finger dexterity. My first typing class in high school was on a manual typewriter. My fingers were strong and fast, and I loved typing class. I had an introduction to shorthand class in high school, and I wanted to learn more. I seemed to have a natural talent for organization. Some people would probably say I have a talent for telling people what to do. I laughed when Tina Fey came out with her book *Bossy Pants*. I guess she had not heard I already had that title. Attending business college allowed me to hone skills I already loved. Miss Hickey's included well-rounded courses in legal and medical terminology, accounting, and even how to develop a professional working wardrobe. The big selling point was a guaranteed job placement upon completion. Executives were standing in line to hire Hickey graduates.

When I was a junior in high school, I met Mike Merrick at the First Baptist Church of Fenton. He and I did not attend the same high schools, so we did not have that in common. He was not as studious as I because he worked after school at a local hamburger stand. I liked Mike. He seemed to be sensible and had a good head on his shoulders. He was tall and handsome with blond hair and a cleft chin. He did not drink or smoke. He told me he was too cheap to waste money on those things. Our friendship was based on a foundation of mutual respect and faith. Of course, friendship developed into romance, and soon, I could not imagine not spending the rest of my life with this man.

During the summer of 1965, I got my first job at Woolworths in Crestwood Plaza. I worked behind the candy counter where we sold a variety of individual pieces of candy that were not already boxed. Customers would make their selection, and I would weigh and bag the candy and calculate the price.

Mike picked me up from work for our first date, and we played miniature golf. As we spent time getting acquainted, we discovered we both liked to bowl. Bowling, going to movies, attending school events, and church were parts of our dating scene. We usually had dinner on Sunday at my parents' house. Mom cooked Sunday dinner, and this continued as a long-standing tradition even after we got married.

Sometimes one just knows something even if you can't explain why. It is like telling a lie and getting that awful feeling in the pit of the stomach. I had a good feeling in the pit of my stomach when it came to Mike. He was respectful to his parents and to my parents. He was and is honest. That is important to me. He didn't brag or put others down. I like to call him my "Steady Eddie."

Since we both attended the same church, we studied the Bible together. Even though we were only teenagers, we believed the decision to get married was to be taken seriously. The Christian covenant of marriage is described in the Bible as "A cord of three strands that is not quickly broken." This verse speaks about how the bond between two people can become even stronger with God at the center of their relationship. The Cord of Three Strands represents the groom, the bride, and the Holy Spirit.

We were married in June of 1967 at the First Baptist Church in Fenton. We had a lovely ceremony with a simple reception in the church basement. I probably would not advise a young couple to get married as young as we did, but it was the right decision for us. After graduating from Miss Hickey's, I accepted a good job with a law firm located in downtown St. Louis. My income allowed

Mike to attend the University of Missouri at St. Louis full-time. I helped proofread Mike's college papers and type them. Both of us believed we were making an investment in our future by staying the course so Mike could receive a bachelor of science in business administration.

Mike is an excellent ping-pong player. He taught me how to play, and playing ping-pong has been part of an after-dinner tradition for many years. There is always a healthy spirit of competition. I like the analogy of playing ping-pong when it comes to learning how to have meaningful conversations. One partner serves and starts the conversation. The other partner returns the serve with a thoughtful response. In ping-pong, this is called a "volley." Volleying is what makes the game of ping-pong challenging, and volleying is what makes for meaningful conversation. Ping-pong is not a game for one person, and neither is having a conversation. Talking with someone is different than slamming an opponent. Trust is developed and nurtured through talking things over and making decisions together. We have shown respect in our marriage by letting each other know every opinion counts.

The house where Linda lived her first year, 1948

Linda playing outside, 1949

Linda Prentice, 1951

Linda with her baby sister, Donna, 1955

Linda's high school graduation photo, 1966

Mike's high school graduation photo, 1965

Mike and Linda show off ping-pong medals

CHAPTER 2:

Mike's Humble Beginnings

"A family is a place where principles are hammered and honed on the anvil of everyday living."

–CHARLES SWINDOLL

My dad, Truman Merrick, did not talk much about his childhood. His parents divorced when he was young, and he never had a relationship with his dad, Paul. His mother, Ethel, did not possess the emotional strength or the finances needed to care for their four sons (Stanley, Joe, Truman, and Perry), and one daughter, Evelyn. My dad and his brothers went to live with an uncle, Noel, who was a farmer in Charleston, Missouri. Uncle Noel was a young widower. His sister-in-law was a nun, Sister Rhoda. Sister Rhoda became Aunt Rhoda when she made the decision to leave the religious order and marry Uncle Noel to help raise his ready-made family. As I remember from the few stories Dad told, his experiences when he lived with Uncle Noel and Aunt Rhoda, affectionately known as "Dodo," were good. My only memory of Aunt Rhoda when I was a young lad is her long-sleeved clothes. She did not roll up her long sleeves when cooking or washing dishes. Of course, Dad and all of his brothers were expected to work hard in the fields, planting and harvesting crops when they were not attending school. Dad said the most he made while working in the fields was fifty cents a day.

My mom, Bertha Angotti, was born in Wirth, Arkansas. Her father, Stephen, and his wife, Margaret, moved their family to Caruthersville, Missouri, where he purchased land to farm and open a blacksmith shop. From what I have been told, his skills and extraordinary strength to lift heavy metal farm implements as he worked in his welding shop were legendary. Even though my grandfather died before I knew him, I felt it was an honor to be named after him. Mom had two older siblings, and when her mother, Margaret, was giving birth to the fourth, she died in childbirth. Stephen Angotti found himself a widower with three young children. He remarried and had two more children with his second wife, Pearl. The siblings may have lived under the same roof, but the stepmother did not treat all the children equally. When the girls in the family were not cooking or working in the fields chopping and picking cotton, they were taught to sew. Bertha's stepmother taught her how to sew, which included quilt making, and hand-stitched detailed, lace needlework called tatting. Mom sewed on an old treadle, Singer sewing machine her entire life. She refused to give it up for a newer model. Quilting was a skill she loved. The hand-stitched quilts she made for the family are some of the best memories we have of her.

My parents married in April 1940, and my older brother, David, was born June 1942. The United States was fighting World War II on two fronts, the South Pacific and Europe. After David was born, Dad was drafted into the Army and served in France. He endured unsanitary conditions, some of which caused trench mouth and the loss of all his teeth. He returned to the United States in poor health. When he arrived, he stood six feet five inches tall and weighed 140 pounds. But, he did return.

MIKE'S EARLY YEARS

I joined the family on a stifling August day in 1947. I was born in Cairo, Illinois, at the closest hospital located across the Mississippi River from East Prairie, Missouri. My five-year-old brother swore they found me on the side of the road and decided to adopt me. All this was said in jest, because my parents wanted another child and had the sincere desire to provide a more stable home environment than either of them had known. It was post-war time, and families and communities craved normalcy.

My parents worked as sharecropper farmers. A sharecropper does not own the land and shares a part of the harvest with the landowner. In some cases, the sharecropper rents the land and pays the landowner a portion of the harvest. The sharecropper pays even if it is a bad harvest year. It would be sixty years before I would eventually realize that my parents, like all farmers, are true business owners and types of entrepreneurs. They planned their work, worked their plan, and then flew by the seat of their pants. They planted their crops and then improvised as the weather changed, equipment broke, or prices changed. Many times, they had to borrow money as they bet that next year would bring an abundant harvest.

In 1951, when I was four years old, my parents had a bumper crop. They decided to sell their farm equipment, pay off their debtors, and move to St. Louis. For many rural families, the big city was pictured as the land of opportunity. My father had heard stories about an abundance of good-paying jobs available in St. Louis. My father completed the eleventh grade but did not graduate from high school. He applied for a job at the General Motors Automobile Plant located off Natural Bridge and Union in north St. Louis. Chevrolet trucks, some cars, including the

Corvette, were built at this facility. Dad was hired and joined the workforce of 3,500 employees. His position was called a stock chaser. It was his responsibility to make sure the auto parts were where they should be. It would be a disaster if the assembly line stopped because parts could not be located or had not been re-stocked. He would retire from this job after more than thirty years. Later in life, when I worked at two separate factories, I started to understand what Dad had given up when he left farming and being his own boss to work in a factory and punch a time clock.

In St. Louis, we lived in city apartments called four- or six-family flats. Growing up, it seemed like we always had family members temporarily living with us as they left farm life and came to the city for better job opportunities. At one point, we had seven relatives living with the four of us in a two-bedroom, one-bath apartment. Some of the adults worked the night shift, and we rotated beds to make the situation work.

HOW MUCH IS $64,000?

In 1955 there was a popular game show, *The $64,000 Question*. One evening, my family was gathered around the twenty-one-inch black and white TV watching the weekly quiz show. The contestant missed the final question and won a new Cadillac as an alternate prize. The contestant said, "Thank you, but I really wanted $64,000." As a kid, I could not understand that prize money could be considered better than a brand-new luxury car. I thought winning a new Cadillac was as good as it could get. I said out loud, "How much is $64,000?" I will never forget my aunt sitting next to me saying, "It is more money than you will ever make." Her expectations of me were quite low. I didn't take offense at her statement, because I didn't know any better. I dare say the adult relatives who lived with us could not imagine making $64,000 either. I had no idea what being poor, middle class, or wealthy even meant. Even though we would probably have been considered poor, we had food, clothes, and a roof over our heads, and our family was happy with the simple things in life.

Having a soda to drink was a real treat growing up. Something as extravagant as a root beer float was relegated to special occasions. I fondly remember a few visits to the local movie theater for a Saturday afternoon matinee. When we were given a soda at home, Mom would make me and my brother, David, divide it 50/50. My older brother, by five years, would get two glasses out of the kitchen cabinet and pour the same amount into each glass. However, he would put more ice cubes in my glass so, even though it appeared we both had the same amount, he would have more. I was not old enough to realize what he had done. It wasn't until years later, he confessed about how he would cheat me, and I was none the wiser.

REAL LIFE MONOPOLY

My brother got a Monopoly Game, which we and all the neighborhood kids loved to play. However, what we did not realize was my brother, as the banker, would mix the bank's money with his money to keep from losing. If he was completely going under, he would fold the Monopoly board and go home. Dave was not a good loser. However, I loved playing Monopoly and still do. I think this is where I first had the desire to own real estate. My family teases me about playing Monopoly for real.

I shared a room with my older brother who was a teenager in the 1950s. He bought the newest 45 RPM record each week.

I went to bed with the latest hit song playing and then woke up with it still playing. I am not very good at trivia, except for 50s music.

I love 1950s music, and when it comes time to get moving and tackle a project I say in my mind or out loud, "It's time to rock 'n' roll." Later in life, my sons were not excited to hear me say on Saturday morning, "It's time to rock 'n' roll!" They knew they would not be sleeping in but working on various manual labor jobs in the family business.

WAGON FOR HIRE

I was about nine years old, and my first money-making venture was collecting old newspapers in my wagon from the neighbors and selling them to a recycling company. I received one dollar for each wagon load I delivered. This job did not last very long because my parents got the idea they could rent a house in southeast Missouri. My parents had a hard time adjusting to the city while living in a cramped apartment, and the lure of returning to the country was always tugging, at Mom's heartstrings in particular.

At one point, Mom, my brother, and I moved to Southeast Missouri, about 200 miles south of St. Louis. Dad continued to work at the Chevrolet plant and drive to the country on weekends. It did not take very long for my parents to realize this was not a good decision. However, this was a decision that was destined to be repeated more than four times. Our family did not like being sep-arated during the week, but Dad could not find a job in Southeast Missouri that would pay as well as his job at the Chevrolet plant. In the 1950s and 1960s and beyond, auto assembly plants offered blue-collar employees top paying jobs with benefits that other employers could not match. While living in the country, I tried picking cotton. I lasted one day. I am sure Forrest Gump would say, "Farm work is hard."

We moved back to St. Louis and returned to the old neighborhood, which was just north of the current Delmar Loop in the city. My parents only rented apartments while living in St. Louis. My mother was always looking for a better apartment, and we moved frequently. My brother and I would joke that the kitchen table had more miles than most cars. As an adult, I would tease my mother that we moved every time the rent was due, but she did not find this humorous.

SCHOOL DAYS

Speaking of the Delmar Loop, if you visit this area of St. Louis, you will see a statue of Chuck Berry, an American singer, guitarist, and songwriter who pioneered rock 'n' roll. Chuck Berry performed once a month at the restaurant and bar, Blueberry Hill, until his death in 2017 at age ninety. As a kid, the lyrics from Berry's song, "School Days," played over in my head repeatedly:

Up in the mornin' and out to school
The teacher is teachin' the Golden Rule
American history and practical math
You study 'em hard and hopin' to pass

I was "up in the morning and out to school" while attending ten different elementary schools between kindergarten and the completion of sixth grade. I started first grade in 1953 and attended Wellston Elementary. In 1954, I attended Dozier Grade School. This year stands out in my memory because one day, I went to school, and, when I returned home that afternoon, we had moved from the second-floor apartment to the first floor of the same apartment building. We moved down the street to a different two-family flat two months later. Some of the schools I attended were like rinse and repeat. My family moved, and I went to a different school and then back to a previous one.

I liked math, and in fourth grade at Dozier Elementary School my teacher, Miss O'Toole, became my all-time favorite grade school teacher. Miss O'Toole gave us flash cards with the multiplication tables on them. This form of learning was helpful to me as I memorized the multiplication tables. She also taught us how to read a map, and studying geography became real and practical. Her teaching method included a simple poem that I bet every kid in the class still remembers:

The top of the map is North,
The bottom of the map is South,
The right is East,
the left is West,
and I never have to guess.

Maps are still the same today, and technology has not completely erased their need.

Spelling is not my strong suit. My spelling is so bad that even Google cannot help me find the correct spelling for a word I am looking for. I experienced a type of motivation to study harder for a spelling test during the months I attended the fifth grade when we were living in Wardell, Missouri.

Remember, it was 1957, and motivation and inspiration were open to interpretation by teachers. Each Friday, we had a spelling test, and, if a student received a grade under seventy-five percent, the student was brought in front of the class and paddled. When I started attending this school, my classmates told me about this, but I thought they were kidding. The first Friday, my spelling grade was below seventy-five percent, but, since I was new, the teacher gave me a pass. However, another kid failed the test and was publicly paddled. I was a believer. Trust me, I never got below seventy-five percent on another spelling test while I attended that school.

Most students in this part of rural Missouri had parents who were farmers. Around April 1, school was suspended for about three weeks so the kids old enough to work in the fields could help. School resumed in May and finished well into June. Mom planned to move back to St. Louis, so she decided I didn't need to go back to the country school in May to finish the school year. I missed almost eight weeks of the last part of the fifth grade. As a result, I failed some classes in sixth grade and had to repeat a portion of this year of school.

I am providing this travelog of my educational experience to help the reader understand the variety of challenges I faced. I don't want to whine about how hard school was, but some areas of study fell through the cracks.

MONEY DOES NOT GROW ON TREES

In December 1959, we moved to Jefferson County, Missouri, about thirty miles from St. Louis City. My parents finally bought a house, allowing us to settle in and put down roots. I was thirteen and in the seventh grade. It was a whole new experience. We had no sidewalks, only gravel streets, and no stores within walking distance. I rode a bus to school for the first time. My brother, Dave, had his driver's license by this time, so he finished high school in St. Louis City. He worked after school and weekends and was gone most of the time.

How many of you have received this speech from your dad? "Son, money doesn't grow on trees." My dad had that one in his pocket, but he had another one that I will give him credit for originality. "Listen up! As fast as I am shoveling money in the front door, this family is carrying it out the back door in teaspoons."

I knew I needed to figure out a way to earn money. My family had a gasoline push lawn mower to cut the grass in our yard. I decided to ask neighbors if I could cut their grass. I developed a good little business, but then I was offered another more appealing job. One of our neighbors owned Kiddie Land, a small amusement park located next to a local shopping center. The rides were similar to what one might see at a fair, but set up in a permanent location and only suitable for younger children. My neighbor hired me to work for him and run the rides. This was my first hourly job paying 50 cents an hour.

Kiddie Land had a miniature Ferris wheel with five cages. I would put the kids in the seats, lock the doors, and start the ride. There was a circular race car track and some arcade games, but the most popular ride consisted of small boats fashioned after speed boats. The colorful boats were in the water but positioned on a track hidden underneath the water, so the kids were not really steering them. The boats were located in a small body of water with a 3-foot-high wall around the outside edge. I was six feet tall and weighed about 120 pounds. I needed to lift the kids over the wall into the boat. A few heavy-weight little kids were a challenge, but I did it with a smile on my face. Even though this job required hard work in the summer heat, it was one of my favorite first jobs.

My reputation as a hard worker spread in the subdivision where we lived. The neighbor who owned Kiddie Land had friends who owned a local public swimming pool. They hired me away from Kiddie Land to work at the swimming pool the following summer. I rode my bike to work because the pool was so close.

The swimming pool was large. It measured 44,000 square feet, about the size of a football field, and held about 1,250,000 gallons of cold spring water. It was a very popular place, and my summers were filled with long hours working behind the counter serving food, cleaning around the pool, and picking up trash. I liked swimming, but it was not as much fun after working all day.

16 CANDLES

In August 1963, I turned sixteen and stood in line to take the much-anticipated driver's test, otherwise known as my ticket to freedom. I passed the driving test. I had wheels because my parents loaned me one of their cars, a 1962 baby-blue Corvair. The Silhouettes song "Get A Job" was playing in my head, and a prospective burger job was on the horizon.

A businessman who attended my church owned a walk-up hamburger stand, Brown's Hamburger Stand, and an IGA grocery store in Fenton. Neal Brown was one of my early business mentors. I respected Neal because he was a hard worker. He kept the grocery store nice and clean and charged fair prices. He was a man of his word and well-respected in the community. In 1963, He hired me to work after school. I worked from five to ten p.m. on Mondays, Tuesdays, Thursdays, Fridays, and eight a.m. until five p.m. on Saturdays. Starting pay was ninety cents an hour. It is not hard to figure out why I was not an A student with a 28-hour work week. We sold hamburgers for fifteen cents, along with French fries, sodas, milk shakes, and malts. The restaurant had a walk-up window with no inside dining. All food was cooked to order the old-fashioned way. Customers could take it to go, sit in their cars, or eat at one of the picnic tables.

Because of my experience with serving food and giving customers the correct change at the swimming pool, I was given the job of waiting on customers as they came up to the counter, I took their orders, their money, and made the correct change. The money in the cash register and the amount on the handwritten ticket stubs had to be balanced at the end of my shift.

After I started working at Brown's, they needed more help. I got my best friend from school, Bill, a job as a fry cook. Later, they hired another friend from school named Hoyet. After he worked at the hamburger stand for a while, he realized he had to pick up the pace during peak hours. We gave him the nickname, "Flash." The name stuck. Both friends were in my wedding, and, when Hoyet was getting fitted for his tuxedo, he told the man his name was Flash.

Bill and I lived about a mile from each other, and I first met him on the school bus. We later got better acquainted by going to school, church, and working together. The school bus picked me up first and then stopped in front of Bill's driveway. Bill's family lived in a trailer. This was my first introduction to a trailer park. Today, a trailer park is usually referred to as a mobile home court. Even though I was only a teenager, I was interested in learning more about business. I found out that most people living in the trailer court owned their mobile homes and rented the concrete pads they set on. Some of the people rented the mobile homes they lived in too. The seeds of investing in real estate and rental income were planted. Little did I realize that about twelve years later, I would buy a 43-pad mobile home court situated on eleven acres named Wheel House Manor. I took the quote from Mark Twain to heart, "Buy land, they aren't making it anymore."

Bill was like most teenage boys who loved fast cars. He had a 1965 4-speed Chevy Impala Super Sport with a modified 327 engine. Teenagers would gather for non-sanctioned drag racing on a two-lane river bottom road. Fortunately, I did not witness any serious accidents during these races. Another popular teenage hangout was the Pacific Drag Racing Track. I would go with other buddies to watch Bill race. Bill still loves to gloat over the nine trophies he won racing.

Bill also had a 1947 refurbished Plymouth sedan. One morning we were on our way to Fox High School. Bill was driving, his brother, Gary, was in the middle, and I was riding shotgun. Of course, no one had seat belts. The two-lane road to high school was hilly and curvy. We were joking and laughing, when suddenly we topped a hill and on the other side was a cab parked in the middle of the road. At the speed we were going, there was no stopping. We smashed into the cab and the car rolled onto the driver's side, sliding down the pavement. I opened the passenger door and crawled out, followed by Gary and Bill. My knee slammed into the door handle with the impact, but none of us had serious injuries. To add insult to injury, as we were standing on the side of the road waiting for the police to show up, our school bus passed, and all the students were hanging out the windows waving and cheering. That 1947 Plymouth was built like a tank and protected three foolish teenagers.

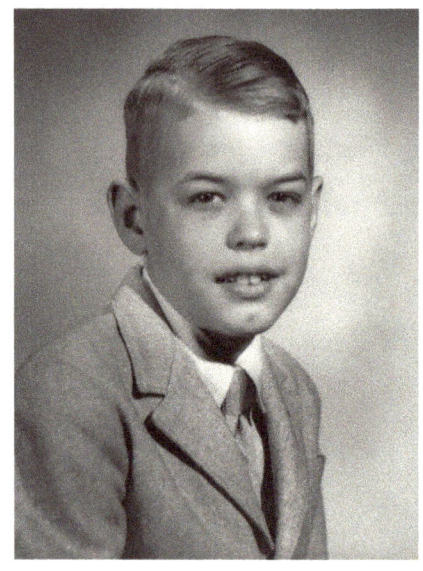

Mike as a child, 1956

Mike and his older brother, David, 1954

The Merrick family still cherishes Bertha's quilts

CHAPTER 3

Love at First Sight

"There will never be anyone else but you."

–RICKY NELSON

I had just turned seventeen and was attending the Youth Group at the First Baptist Church in Fenton, where I met the girl who would be my future wife, Linda Prentice. With my work schedule, I did not date very much, but, for me, it was love at first sight.

We went to the same church, but we attended different high schools. Linda was a straight-A student. I was a straight-C student, at best. Linda was the type of student who teachers loved. She played the flute in the school orchestra and played in the marching band. She took drama and acted in school plays. She was a member of the National Honor Society (NHS). One day, she told me she had an after-school meeting of the NHS to attend. I said, "What is the National Honor Society?" I am thankful she did not laugh at me, but we have laughed about this together through the years.

We began to date and became good friends. We did not have the same academic rankings but enjoyed spending time together. We had a foundation of common faith, trusted each other, and fell in love. When we were dating, I drove a 1962 Chevrolet Corvair that leaked oil. As a general rule, all Corvairs leaked oil or were out of oil, so I thought nothing about it. Because our street and driveway were gravel, I did not notice the leak. However, Linda's driveway was concrete and spotless. On my first visit to her house, I parked in the driveway. When her father saw the oil spot on his driveway, he told her to tell me to park on the street, and I do not think he was smiling when he told her.

COLLEGE YEARS

I graduated from high school in June of 1965. High school graduates, at the time, were told a college degree sealed your future. I never considered going away to college. My parents could not offer any funding, and I knew I had to work part-time to pay for college. Most of my high school buddies and I enrolled at the new community college, Jefferson College in Hillsboro, Missouri, which we called Jeffco. We had no idea that going to college and going to high school was going to be so different. One by one, my friends dropped out. By the end of the first semester, my best friend, Bill, had quit college and joined the Navy. He was gone for the next four years. I continued to attend community college, even though it was a struggle to maintain a two-point grade average. I really had not focused on schoolwork or developed good study habits in high school. Now, I was carrying fifteen hours in college and working twenty-five to thirty hours a week. This could be the reason I still have dreams that I am unable to complete my finals, and I don't graduate from college.

I left Brown's Hamburger Stand in 1966 to work at Greif Brothers, an industrial packaging company. This job was my first experience working in a factory. It was also when I realized what my father had given up as a farmer to go to work inside a car assembly plant. One week after I started to work at Greif Brothers, the union went on strike for a 5-cents-an-hour pay increase. I knew a little about how long strikes could last because my dad was a member of the United Auto Workers (UAW). I didn't have any cash reserves on hand, so I took another job at American Can Company. They put me on the day shift my first week, but then I was switched to the night shift and, finally, to the third shift, midnight to eight a.m. I realized working on an assembly line and making lids for cans was not for me. There was no way I could go to college and work the night shift when the fall semester started.

Neal Brown asked me to come back to work for him as manager of the Brown's Hamburger Stand. I took this job and attended night school at the college. As a manager, I was responsible for all aspects of running the restaurant. This job included inventory control, bank deposits, hiring, firing, plus working the day shift. Neal Brown was an interesting person in that he had been a bomber pilot over Germany in World War II. A picture of Neal and his plane hung on the wall in his office, but he never spoke about that part of his life. He came back after the war, went into the grocery store business, married, and had five children. He liked me and treated me like I was a son. He turned me loose to run the business as if it were my own.

I quickly learned working with and managing those same employees is totally different. I didn't think I changed, but what changed was how they viewed me when I was in charge. This life lesson has continued as I managed people and became a business owner. We may not want it to be this way, but there is a hierarchy in business. Even if you are a business owner with only one employee, the owner cannot be best buddies with the employees. The owner can respect and support employees in every way possible. Keep in mind, in the workplace, it's more important to be a boss than to be a friend. Being too friendly can jeopardize your authority.

The baby boom generation started in 1946, a year before I was born. In the 1960s, I was managing baby boomers born in the early 1950s. These teenagers had a good work ethic. I never worried about whether someone would show up for work, even for an entry-level job.

Since Neal Brown also owned five IGA Grocery Stores, I was able to get the supplies for the hamburger stand from his stores. When I went to pick up supplies, I started talking to one of the store's managers who was about fifty-five years old. During the conversation, he said he used to own his own store. I asked, "Why would you give that up to be a store manager?" He said his store made money, but the pressure of being an owner was too much. His doctor told him, if he didn't change, he would be dead. As a nineteen-year-old I really did not understand. He then said," Mike, all the money in the world does you no good if you are constantly stressed and unable to enjoy life." I remembered these words a few years later when I realized how important it is to set priorities for worship, family, work, and play.

*"To change your life,
you need to change your priorities."*

–MARK TWAIN

PARTNERSHIP IN LOVE AND BUSINESS

On June 17, 1967, at age nineteen, I married my best friend and the love of my life. Linda graduated from high school when she was seventeen. The following year, we decided to get married. Later, we would say we raised each other.

Mike and Linda married, 1967

Mike and Linda leaving their wedding, 1967

CHAPTER 4:

College Versus Real World Experience

"Genius is one percent inspiration and ninety-nine percent perspiration."

-THOMAS EDISON

By the time we married in 1967, Linda had graduated from Miss Hickey's Business School. Linda had some good jobs as an executive assistant and made more money than I did, even after I graduated from college. She was committed to supporting us, as much as possible, so I would not drop out of college. We lived in a one-bedroom apartment in St. Louis County, and I transferred to Meramec Junior College, graduating with an associate's degree.

While I continued to manage Brown's Hamburger Stand, Mr. Brown bought a second restaurant, Dog 'n' Suds in Arnold. This location had car hops, which was a whole new management experience. I told Linda more than once, "I swear, the pants the car hops wear are painted on." The mathematical equation: Tight pants = more tips.

In the fall of 1969, I stopped working for Mr. Brown to attend the University of Missouri at St. Louis (UMSL) full-time. They had a highly-ranked business degree program, and Linda and I decided it was time to put all my effort into completing my bachelor of science in business administration with a minor in accounting. Linda helped proofread my essay papers and typed them. We believed we were investing in our future.

Linda's parents, Henry and Edna, were proprietors of their restaurant called the Hi-Way House in Fenton. They started leasing the building in 1957 when it was directly accessible off the historic Route 66, and it was a popular tourist stop. In 1959, the highway was expanded with additional lanes and became Interstate 44. The restaurant was now positioned off a service road. On paper, everything indicated a significant reduction in tourist traffic because motorists would need to take an exit about one mile before they could see the restaurant. At the same time, the door was being shut or partially shut to tourist patrons, another door was about to swing wide open to approximately 1500 auto workers at the newly completed Chrysler Plant located within a stone's throw of the Hi-Way House.

My mother-in-law, Edna, opened the restaurant at 5 a.m. Monday through Saturday to serve breakfast. My father-in-law, Henry, came in at 10 a.m. for the lunch rush, and worked until 10 p.m. or later to close the restaurant. They had a full staff of waiters, cooks, and bartenders. On Friday night, when the Chrysler workers got paid, the workers would arrive with their weekly paychecks and wanted to get them cashed. In those days, direct deposit didn't exist. Henry decided, for a small fee, to be their banker, so to speak. Check cashing made the customers happy, and they spent more money on food and drinks. The Chrysler workers had thirty minutes to leave their job, drive to the restaurant, cash their checks, get something to eat and drink, then get back to the assembly plant and back on the job. The car plant workers arrived first, and later, the truck plant workers arrived.

They hired me, their new son-in-law, to be the check cashier. Back in the late 1960s, we were cashing at least $20,000 of payroll checks. In 2024 dollars, this amount would be about $200,000 worth of check cashing in one hour. My father-in-law kept a loaded pistol under the counter by the cash register. Thankfully, no one ever tried to rob us.

My in-laws, like my parents, lived through the depression years. They were hard workers and generous as well. One day after the noon rush hour at the restaurant, there was a knock on the back door. There stood a man about thirty-five years old, poorly dressed, and he asked for something to eat. Henry went and got the man a big plate of food, a fork and knife, and something to drink. The unkempt man sat on the back steps of the restaurant and started to eat. After he was finished, he knocked on the door again, handed the plate back and thanked Henry. He never asked for money, just something to eat. I made some snide comment about, "Why doesn't he go get a job?" Henry said, "You don't understand." He was right. I had a lot to learn, and actions *do* speak louder than words.

My father-in-law knew Linda and I needed extra money for me to be able to finish college. He overpaid me for the number of hours I worked. He treated me like a son and became my best friend and mentor. While working at the Hi-Way House, I learned how a full-scale restaurant operates. I never cooked, but I waited on tables. Since I did not like the taste of alcohol or beer, I made the perfect bartender because there was no shrinkage. In college I learned theory, and Henry taught me business in real life.

I continued to work a few hours while attending UMSL until I received my diploma. I was a student who struggled with the traditional classroom setting. I am more of a hands-on learner.

I liked it when some of the professors were honest enough to close the books and speak from their hearts about their real-life experiences. While I was grateful for those professors, they were in the minority. I will never forget an instructor my senior year in college who said, "If you are not in the top ten percent of the class, you have just wasted the last four years."

Later, when my company, Fish Window Cleaning Services, became successful and received several recognitions, I was invited to speak during an UMSL alumni luncheon. I told them the story about the professor who had put down those students whose grade point averages were less than the top tier students and suggested they should consider treating C students with more respect. Needless to say, I did not receive the round of applause I hoped for that day. I wish I had seen this particular episode of "Late Night" with David Letterman before I prepared my speech. Tom Hanks was Letterman's guest and after bantering about Tom's recent movie, the conversation moved to elementary and high school experiences. Both men discovered they were not great students and were pretty much bored with the standard curriculum. Each man was told by more than one teacher that they would never amount to anything. Letterman stood from behind his desk and Tom rose from his chair and they leaped into the air with their hands meeting and cried, "Here's to all the 'C' students in the world." I do not dismiss the prowess of intellectuals, but I love the famous quote attributed to Thomas Edison:

"Genius is one percent inspiration and ninety-nine percent perspiration."

CHAPTER 5:

Sheepskin and Suits

*"Financial peace isn't the acquisition of stuff.
It's learning to live on less than you make,
so you can give money back and
have money to invest."*

–DAVE RAMSEY

In 1971, I graduated from college with a fair amount of perspiration, earning a diploma with a major in business administration and a minor in accounting. An article in a St. Louis newspaper said 1971 was the worst time for college graduates to get a job since the Great Depression. Jobs were hard to find. My wife's Aunt Vesta worked at Farm and Home Savings and Loan, which received its Charter in 1893 and had offices in Missouri and Texas.

Aunt Vesta put in a good word for me, and, after an interview, I was hired to work in the downtown St. Louis branch office. I was happy to have a job, however, I went to work making a lower salary than I did working as the manager of Brown's Hamburger Stand.

My entry position at Farm and Home Savings and Loan was as an assistant manager at their downtown office where I opened new savings accounts for customers. Soon after starting, the long-term manager at the office developed health problems, and I became the working manager.

At this time, all branch managers were men and all tellers were women. The company had a strict policy for managers. If you were a manager, you did not do the work of a teller or vice versa. In my opinion, this was not a good rule. Upper management did not seem to understand the importance of the tellers. I would watch as customers lined up to be waited on by their favorite tellers. The customer probably needed the same basic service, but if the teller remembered their name or asked about their children or dog, the customer was willing to wait in a longer line. Eventually, I have had the privilege of managing employees in my own business. I try to teach customer service techniques to improve the customer's experience. If employees treat customers with politeness and respect, this will go a long way in retaining loyal customers.

In 1973, I was promoted to assistant secretary and branch manager of the South County Office. Most of my job consisted of opening accounts for new and existing customers. I loved talking with people and most of them loved telling me their life stories. They would tell me about companies they worked for or businesses they had developed. They shared work philosophies and gave me insight into how they achieved their wealth.

I learned there were basically four categories of wealthy people who would sit down at my desk to open accounts:

1. Some customers had old money either through inheritance or marriage.
2. Some had high paying jobs, such as doctors, lawyers, and top executives.
3. Some were savers. These people lived below their income and consistently saved money over time.
4. Some were business owners. These people had invested in a business or businesses and were their own bosses.

I knew I did not fall into the first two categories. I planned to be in the third category by saving along the way. I was drawn, however, to the idea of having a business of my own. I was always thinking about possible future business opportunities. The first major goal, though, was to move from our one-bedroom apartment to a house. My father-in-law owned an acre of ground, which he bought as an investment. He told us we could have this acre, and he helped us finance building a house. Initially, I could not pay much more than a small amount of principal with interest. I was more the recipient of this arrangement, but Henry was pleased to earn a decent amount of interest from his cash reserves.

THE BUSINESS OF TAXES

In 1973, Linda and I met a friend at church, Larry. In one of our conversations, he told me about his mother who had her own tax and bookkeeping business. I decided to meet with her to find out more. After our meeting, I believed this was an idea for a home-based business I could work on at night to supplement my income. She said the best way to learn how to prepare taxes is to go to the H&R Block Tax School. For a reasonable fee, they taught students how to prepare tax returns and then offered the opportunity to work for them at night during tax season. I enrolled in the next class. Linda also took the training a year later.

Since I am a hands-on type of learner, I liked the way the instructor taught. With the foundation I already had from my college accounting classes, I was a fast learner, and I really liked doing personal and small business taxes. This training was not just theory like college; this was the real world. The instructor and I became friends, and upon graduation from H&R Block

Tax School, he hired me to work in his office at night to prepare tax returns.

I became an immediate hit with family and friends by doing their taxes for free. I learned most people were scared to death of the IRS and had no idea how to read or complete tax forms. The average person did not understand tax deductions. All they knew was at the end of the year, they either owed money or they got a refund. Most did not understand that, usually, receiving a refund reflected their overpayment of taxes. While doing their taxes, I was asked the same questions repeatedly:

- My son or daughter is getting married; can I deduct expenses?
- My relative just moved in with us for three months, can I deduct them as a dependent?
- A relative died, and I helped with the funeral expenses. Is this tax deductible?

When I immediately came back with the answer, they thought I was a walking tax manual, not realizing the last person asked the same or similar questions.

While still working at Farm and Home Savings and Loan, and, after two seasons of working for H&R Block, I opened my own tax and bookkeeping business. I prepared monthly ledgers for a few small businesses: Three gas stations, a beauty salon, a pet supply store, and a construction company. I provided monthly profit and loss statements for the businesses and filed the quarterly and year-end taxes. I also prepared taxes for individuals. My clientele grew from referrals. I met with the customers, completed the Federal and Missouri tax forms by hand, and Linda typed the forms and made carbon paper copies.

BABY BLESSINGS

Linda and I were married for seven years before we welcomed our first son, Matthew, in June 1974. We brought him home from the hospital on Father's Day, also our seventh wedding anniversary. Matt was passed around by grandparents and a multitude of doting relatives who came to visit.

Linda wanted to stop working full-time outside the home and stay home with Matt. She was still earning more than I was, so cutting our income in half was a big decision. However, our tax business was growing, and she could do this from home.

CHOICES MAKE A DIFFERENCE

One Sunday, Linda was sick, and I went to church by myself. I don't remember what the sermon was about, but it was as if the Lord was speaking directly to me, saying, "Mike, you are prideful about money and possessions." This made me realize I needed to prioritize what I really valued in life. This has been a life-long lesson I am still learning. In a nutshell, people are more important than things. If I put boundaries around my desires to have bigger and better houses, cars, or expensive hobbies, I could give more to church, charities, and support for people and organizations that make a difference.

I was tested on my resolve, because I really wanted to get my pilot's license. I had a couple of friends who had their pilot's licenses and owned small airplanes. One of these friends, Kenny, was certified to teach at a regional airport in Fenton. I took the ground school classroom training, flight school, and achieved the qualifications to fly solo. I love the memory of the day I soloed with all the jumbled emotions of apprehension and exhilaration.

I'm glad I had this experience and have loved flying with others in small planes as a passenger. I could not afford this expensive hobby without putting a financial strain on the rest of the family. Instead, I decided to pursue simpler pastimes such as bike riding, camping, and fishing. Gratefully, I never regretted this decision.

Mike and Linda's parents
at Mike's college graduation, 1971

Mike's college graduation, 1971

Mike's promotion to bank manager, 1973

Matt's first day home from the hospital,
June 1974

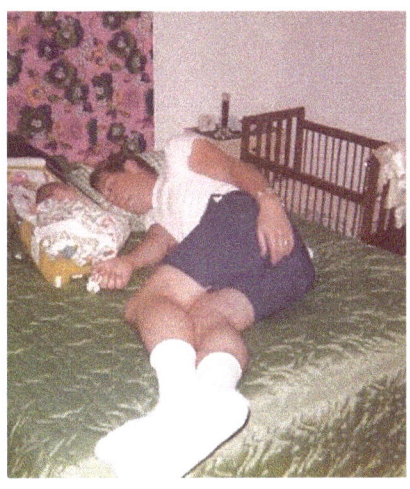

Mike and Matt needed a nap

CHAPTER 6:

A Big Move

"Be grateful and you won't grumble.
Grumble and you won't be grateful."

–BILLY GRAHAM

As I continued working at Farm & Home Savings, my thoughts kept returning to ideas for owning my own business. Each day after work, I drove past a trailer court, Wheel House Manor Mobile Home Park, which reminded me of the trailer court where my buddy, Bill, lived when he was in high school. I always thought it was an interesting business concept. One day I saw a For Sale sign in front of the park. I stopped and talked to the owner, Ed. He told me the price, and I went home and told Linda. I explained that by investing in real estate, we would have rental income, which would provide a way for us to raise a family without her working outside the home. With fear and trembling, I dropped the bombshell, "If we sell our house, we will have enough money for the down payment!" We both said, "Let's pray about it." After prayer and contemplation, we decided to purchase the mobile home court. It still amazes me she was willing to give up a custom-built home to follow this business idea of mine.

We used the funds after the sale of the house to put a down payment on the mobile home park, a forty-three-pad mobile home court situated on eleven acres in Fenton. We then moved from a three-bedroom ranch home on an acre of ground into a

12' x 65' mobile home at 104 Wheel House Manor. My parents, my in-laws, and most of my friends thought we had lost our minds. At the time, we did not know Linda was pregnant with our second child. The mobile home was shrinking fast! I already used a spare bedroom as an office to manage the mobile home court and to continue my tax and bookkeeping service. Now, we needed a third bedroom for a nursery. In August 1976, we were blessed with our second son, Nathan.

My father-in-law, who was not only a great cook and restaurant owner, was a carpenter at heart. He came to our rescue and said, "I think we can build a house on the backside of the mobile home court." This section of our property was about two acres with a very steep slope. It was not ideal land, but we decided we could make it work because we definitely needed more living space for the four of us. We found an architect who drew up plans, and we estimated what we thought the cost would be if we did most of the work. I helped as much as possible on days off and on the weekends. We found a man, Griff, then on strike from the Chrysler plant, who had some carpentry experience. We hired him, and we did all the framework, plumbing, brick work, and roofing. I got a crash course on how to build a house. Since we did most of the work ourselves and bought supplies such as good used lumber, we were able to keep the building costs at $30,000.

When we bought the mobile home court, the tenants' pad rent generated income. Water, trash and sewer were included in the pad rental. I learned I could make the business more profitable by buying a mobile home when it went up for sale. I could collect rent from the tenant who occupied the mobile home as well as the pad rent. Of course, there was more involved than just purchasing a mobile home. Most required some amount of rehabbing and ongoing maintenance. Maintenance included sealing roof tops, repairing the skirting, and fixing air conditioners. Mobile homes are prone to problems with plumbing, especially in cold weather. Water pipes can freeze even if they are well insulated. I have crawled under many mobile homes to disassemble a frozen water line and thaw it out. My coat would freeze to the ground as I lay on my back, working on the pipes. At one time, I owned twenty-five rentals in the court. Linda, our two young sons, and my in-laws helped me maintain these properties in various ways. Wheel House Manor Mobile Home Court was truly a family business.

I did not have a great attitude about working at Farm and Home. I did not like wearing a suit and tie daily and working on Saturdays. I still had the loan to pay off for the mobile home court, and I could not walk away from my full-time job. The Bible has many verses about being grateful. Over time, I really did have an attitude adjustment about my job. Bad attitudes are not isolated. Perhaps I was hiding my attitude about work while working, but my complaints carried over to home. I did not want this to continue. I did not want to live with the idea that the grass was always greener elsewhere. When I counted my blessings, especially being thankful for a loving wife and two healthy sons, my pettiness started to melt away.

Wheel House Manor Mobile Home Court aerial view 1976

House we built on property that was
part of Wheel House Manor 1976

Matt meets baby brother, Nathan,
on first day home August 1976

CHAPTER 7:

Windows of Opportunity

"The Lord opened a window of opportunity that was taller and wider than I could imagine."

–MIKE MERRICK

In the fall of each year, Farm and Home would have a big bushel basket full of candy-red apples in the lobby for customers to take. Usually, we would get the apples shipped in, but, for whatever reason, our shipment did not arrive, and I had to find a bushel of apples. I went to Sappington Market, and as I was buying the apples, Mark Stobie, the window cleaner for Farm and Home, was there. We started talking, and he said he was meeting someone who wanted to purchase his window cleaning business, but that person had not shown up.

Always looking at business opportunities, I said, "I might be interested." He was very skeptical. I was a white-collar banker saying I wanted to consider buying a window cleaning business. I made an appointment with him to look at his books later that week. With my background in taxes and accounting, the business looked like a good opportunity financially.

After looking at the books, and I use that term loosely, I asked about his expenses because his books consisted of a handwritten list of approximately one hundred commercial window cleaning accounts. Mark was like many one-man businesses. He was vague about expenses, but I could estimate his overhead was his labor, a vehicle, and some equipment.

I went home and told Linda about the business. Remember, we were do-it-yourself-type people. After all, we had just built our own house. Her words to me were, "Who in the world pays to have their windows cleaned?" I explained that commercial businesses do, "The businesses are not high-rises. Mark cleans businesses like Farm and Home Savings and retail businesses like banks, restaurants, and day care centers. I think this is an interesting service business. It is unlike the restaurant business with high overhead, inventory, and all the headaches. It has low overhead, and there is no need to work nights or on weekends." I was really selling the idea to Linda.

I decided to go out with Mark on my day off and see how I liked window cleaning. I think he thought I was just wasting his time. I'm sure he did not think I would buy the business. He looked at me as free labor and was going to take advantage of an extra pair of hands as much as possible. He had me carry the equipment and do the grunt work, while he showed me his window cleaning techniques.

After that day of pretending to be a window cleaner, I prayed about what to do. Should I step out and buy the window cleaning business or stay at what I thought was a secure job with Farm and Home Savings? Annual raises were due in January, and I prayed for direction. I thought, "If I get a good raise, I will stay at Farm and Home, and, if not, I will quit and buy the window cleaning business."

The answers to prayers can arrive special delivery in packages different than we might expect. My boss came in that fateful day in January to tell us about raises. As I awaited what I thought would be an announcement of a salary increase, it turned out to be a pronouncement. He told me, "Mike, we are cutting back on payroll, and we are starting with you. You are fired. Clean out your desk." Some people try to soften it by saying, "We are letting you go." No, I was fired, and there was no going back. I have reflected on that day with humility. I had never been fired before, and it was a blow to the ego. This experience helped me bond over the years with many other members of this club, made up of fired employees. I was also filled with gratitude. I prayed for direction, and God put a flashing green light in my path. I don't believe I can take credit for the decision to purchase the window cleaning business. The Lord opened a window of opportunity that was taller and wider than I could imagine.

GREEN LIGHT

I don't want to make it sound as if I was dripping with confidence. Arriving at home in the middle of the day with my wife and two young sons wondering why Daddy is home so early was terrifying. I told Linda our answered prayer was perhaps not as gentle as we might have imagined, but it was an answer. I would not be going back to Farm and Home Savings. I told her I wanted to buy Mark's Window Cleaning Business. The conversation then focused on our core family belief: Prioritizing quality time together. Since Linda had grown up with her parents working long hours in the restaurant, we asked ourselves the question that still resonates today, "Can we own a business without it owning us?"

We concluded that managing a service business that operated during daytime hours and not weekends would be family friendly. I called Mark and said, "I want to buy your business."

Mark earned $13,500 a year in gross revenue, while I was paid $13,000 annually as a banker. I thought to myself, "I just got a $500 a year raise!" Not realistic thoughts for a business major since I didn't factor the expenses of doing business.

The next day I went to Boatmen's Bank to get the cashier's check to buy the business. This is the bank I went to each day while working at Farm and Home to make the daily deposits. They asked why I needed the check, and I explained I was purchasing a window cleaning business. The bank manager took me into his private office and said, "If you do not drip water on my wooden parquet floors, you can have this job." I was walking on cloud nine. I was growing my business on day one! I could envision how this business could grow, job by job, grasping a bit of the opportunity that lay ahead. One of my own personal quotes is, "Every piece of glass you see will be cleaned by someone." From early on, I knew I wanted that someone to be me and my company.

I immediately left the bank with a cashier's check in hand and scheduled a meeting with Mark. I will never forget his encouraging words to me. He took the check for $3,200, looked at it, folded it up, put it in his pocket and said, "Mike, you think you know what you're doing, but you don't." And with those words of encouragement, we went out on my second and last day of training.

We had cleaned about fifteen percent of his customers. Instead of introducing me to the rest of his customers, he handed me a sheet of paper with the customers' names, addresses, the cleaning frequency, and whether cash was collected or the service invoiced. As we drove past businesses, Mark made comments about the job, and I was writing as quickly as possible to help remember what he was saying.

It was January 1978, and snow was predicted for St. Louis. I said, "If it snows, I hope it will stick on the ground until the weekend so I can take the boys sledding." He said, "You are crazy." I guess it had not sunk in that I would not be sitting behind a desk in a nice warm office anymore. I got my wish, and that year St. Louis set a record for continuous days with snow on the ground… fifty-two days without significant melting. The boys and I did a lot of sledding that year, and I did a lot of slip-sliding around as I learned how to clean windows. My experiences while cleaning windows have given me a real appreciation for our hard-working window cleaners across the country who brave all kinds of weather.

CHAPTER 8:

Fish Window Cleaning is Born

*"Perseverance is the hard work
you do after you get tired of doing
the hard work you already did."*

–NEWT GINGRICH

Linda and I discussed what name we should call our new window cleaning business. Mike's Window Cleaning would have been similar to Mark's Window Cleaning, but that did not seem right. I needed to clean windows to get the business going, but I had a vision to grow it beyond one person. I was passionate about working hard and making it the premier window cleaning company, at least in St. Louis.

I believed the Lord answered my prayer and put me in the window cleaning business. Linda and I decided to name the business Fish Window Cleaning. The story goes that in Biblical times, if Christians met and did not know each other, they basically had a secret code. One person would take his staff and draw what would look like a half circle in the sand, and if the other person were a Christian, he would draw the other half and cross the end to look like a fish. The Greek word for fish is "ichthys," and, in early years, our business cards had the symbol of the fish with the Greek letters inside. Our first tagline was "Don't Get Caught with Dirty Windows."

Over the years, when people ask where the name came from, if they are interested, I tell them the story. Had I named the business Mike's Window Cleaning, we probably would not have been able to trademark the name. The name Fish Window Cleaning was available to be trademarked in Missouri and eventually in all fifty states. We are Fish Window Cleaning®.

WINDOW CLEANER REALITY

Honestly, nothing prepared me for my first day on the job by myself. On my first day, I picked the largest job on the customer list. I am still not sure why. It was a two-story office building. It was snowing, and I probably thought I needed a job that had interior glass to be cleaned. I was cleaning an inside office with glass partitions. When I pulled my pole back, it hit a large flower vase and knocked it over, leaving broken pieces in a pile on the floor. Panic set in. I figured I was already in the hole dollar-wise, and I had not even finished my first job. Thankfully, this was not a family heirloom, and I could buy a replacement vase that made the client happy. It was a lesson I learned early on to be super careful, especially when working inside. It was also a lesson that helped me be a better employer when window cleaners would come into my office and tell me they accidentally broke something. I could be firm but also sympathetic as I admonished the cleaner to be more careful.

The two-story office building, which was my first big window cleaning job, took me about fifty hours to clean inside and outside the first time. I learned a lot about what makes the customer happy. First, the building had aluminum frames around the glass entrance and the customer was insistent about the frames being cleaned as well as the windows. I learned it is important to do a good job, and this can best be achieved by listening to customers and concentrating on cleaning the areas they deem to be a priority.

The great thing about the longevity of window cleaning is those same windows still get dirty forty-five years later. My grandson, Sam, and another crew member cleaned the same windows on the same building, which was my first job, in a fraction of the time. Sam had better tools and much better training!

About a year after I started, I ran into Mark Stobie, and he asked how I was doing with the window cleaning business. I told him that I was scheduled to clean about $30,000 for the year. His exact words back to me, "NO WAY!" I said, "Yes, I am pretty sure $30,000." He just could not believe it. He kept saying, "There is NO WAY you can clean that much glass." When I got home that night, I refigured the numbers and I *was* on schedule to clean a little more than $30,000 worth of windows.

I cleaned windows during the week and with my father-in-law's help, we maintained the mobile home court and the rental mobile homes I owned. Matt and Nathan, our sons, grew up in a family business. The mobile home court had all types of manual labor jobs for which training began at an early age. They could help sweep the street of debris and assist with mixing and pouring concrete to patch holes in the street or expand driveways. Remembering the music of my youth, I would start the Saturday workday by saying, "OK boys; it's time to rock 'n' roll." In short, we all pitched in if there was a project that had to be done.

As Matt and Nathan got older, they began to help with window cleaning jobs. They usually joined me for on-the-job training on Saturday mornings or when they had days off school. Some challenging jobs we tackled together were special requests to remove various holiday paint designs on storefronts. Anyone who has ever cleaned windows will understand what I mean when I say there was a day of rejoicing when spray snow went out of favor. That stuff was almost impossible to remove. When they became young men, they had extensive experience cleaning windows. Other employees had to respect that Dad didn't give them token jobs, but they earned their place and were very good window cleaners who eventually became integral parts of the franchise business.

In the early years, FISH business cards had the Christian fish symbol with Greek letters

Mike wearing a Fish Window Cleaning hat, 1978

CHAPTER 9:

Window by Window

*"A successful man is one who can lay
a firm foundation with the bricks that
others throw at him."*

–JIM ROHN

Early on, I picked up new business when customers would stop me while I was cleaning a business next to theirs and ask if I could start cleaning their business. This sales tactic took me from $13,500 to about $30,000+ at the close of my first business year. I realized that to grow the business to a level I believed was possible, I needed to cold-call. Cold-calling requires walking into local businesses and asking if I could offer a free estimate for regular window cleaning. It takes some moxie to cold-call, but I was not strong-arming anyone. Smart business owners recognized clean windows are the first thing customers see and notice. I offered reliable service backed by liability insurance and a quality guarantee. It did not take long before I had more business than I could clean by myself. After about six months, I hired my first employee and soon after, my second employee.

ORGANIZATIONAL CHARTS CANNOT BE LINEAR

I was still cleaning windows, and with larger jobs, I cleaned side-by-side with my employees. However, I quickly learned that *managing* my employees was different; I had transitioned to business owner, and my employees related to me differently. I was not just another employee who was one level above, but I was viewed as the "filthy rich business owner." After all, the owner signs the paychecks and most likely has a large hidden stash of cash. This perception is a lesson I have tried to share with other business owners and eventually our franchisees. Business owners need a buffer in the organizational chart. Hiring a manager to supervise employees is a critical investment for growth. In other words, employees will listen to another employee who is their supervisor.

As the business grew, I thought this would be a great business to franchise, even though I knew nothing about the ins and outs of franchising. All businesses have some type of glass that needs cleaning, and this was not unique to businesses in St. Louis. What would it be like to open another Fish Window Cleaning in a different city? I pondered this dream for almost twenty years before the time was right to figure out how to franchise.

BRICK WALLS

I had steady, consistent growth with the window cleaning business. However, I would experience obstacles like losing a good employee or a good-paying customer, and production would slide backward. Sometimes, these obstacles felt more like hitting a brick wall. I describe a brick wall as some situation that, at the time, seems impossible.

One of the first walls was trying to grow the business beyond $100,000 in annual production. It is important to point out that, at this time, everything was done manually. It took considerable time to organize and document everything on paper without computers. I did all employee hiring, kept employee documentation, handled payroll, and paid quarterly taxes. I scheduled the commercial jobs and organized which jobs would be cleaned by which window cleaner.

For the first ten years, I only had commercial window cleaning customers. I answered the phone and took care of customer complaints, which were, thankfully, few. As I crossed the $100,000 projection, something caused a decline. This continued for at least a year. I did not understand the importance of hiring more window cleaners than you think you will need because not all employees work to their full potential.

I should have learned this lesson from my brother, Dave, who was the night plant manager at the Ford Assembly Plant in Hazelwood, Missouri. To keep the car assembly line running to capacity, especially on Mondays or Fridays, they needed at least ten percent more employees to pull from the employee pool because employees would not show up for work, leave early, or just slack off. I thought this was only true in a manufacturing setting, but it is also true in a service business.

MORE EMPLOYEES = MORE SALES

If I wanted to grow, I needed to hire more window cleaners than I thought I needed. It is a hard concept to grasp, and, in later years, it has been a hard concept for franchisees. An optimistic business owner will see there is an unlimited amount of glass needing cleaning, and it is prudent to hire extra workers to cover the demand. I decided to try to hire enough window cleaners to get all the work done. As more cleaners were on the street, Fish Window Cleaning became more visible, and more window cleaning jobs came in exponentially. As I started to hire more employees, I quickly passed the $100,000 mark.

OVER HIRE – OVER HIRE – OVER HIRE

In the late 1980s, most of my new hires were in their twenties and part of a new generation of employees. Many of the workers I hired were interested in a certain lifestyle. They wanted to make good money but also liked taking an afternoon or a day off. Employee performance dictated the pay schedule. FISH paid the window cleaner a percentage of the gross revenue they produced. Much to my surprise, instead of working longer to get more jobs and make more money, they preferred to stop working early or take Friday off to do something they liked. After an employee worked for about a month, I estimated how much the window cleaner was going to clean. Put another way, if the cleaner reached their income goal in thirty hours, they stopped working for that week. I stopped listening to what they said they were going to do and looked, instead, at what they actually did. I stopped being frustrated as I learned to adjust my expectations and adapt from there. The employees were happy, and I finally hired enough workers to continue to grow. During this growth cycle, I also hired an administrative assistant to help answer the phones, schedule cleanings, and manage billing.

BLUE FISH, GREEN FISH, RED FISH, YELLOW FISH

Scheduling and keeping track of jobs was really a challenge. One day, an employee suggested putting the jobs on index cards. A simple solution to a complex problem. I went out and bought five sets of index cards. Blue for week one, green for week two, red for week three, and yellow for week four. White was used for a monthly or project job or a house. As silly as this may sound, it was simple and easy and worked beautifully. If, for some reason, the work in one week was not done, a red card readily stood out in a yellow week. Folks still kid me about running my entire business on index cards, but this concept took us all the way from the late '70s until we started using computers in the mid-'90s.

Fish Window Cleaning was growing, and I was excited about the potential. Running into another brick wall was long overdue, but it came in a way I was not expecting. Around 1994, my manager, and also my best window cleaner, came to me and suggested I bring him on as a partner. I respected him as a good employee, but I was not going to create a partnership. He was angry when I did not go for his idea, and the best way to get back at me was to leave and start his own window cleaning company, taking two other cleaners with him.

This was a dark day for me, and I honestly considered reducing my workforce and cleaning windows myself again. Many, if not all, small business owners have similar thoughts when key employees quit. Michael Gerber talks about this in his book, *The E-Myth*. When I read this book, it was comforting to know I was not alone in thinking I should make my business small again. *The E-Myth* describes a business owner's challenges around hiring and keeping a workforce. This is just a fact. I did not have a problem getting more window cleaning accounts. I had to decide whether to stay small or grow. Fortunately, the thought of going back and being the main window cleaner with only one or two employees did not last more than a couple of days. I immediately started to rehire and rebuild. The amount of glass that needed to be cleaned had not changed, and I was hopeful I could find good, loyal employees.

RUN IT UP THE FLAGPOLE

I still had the idea that it was possible to replicate the window cleaning business in other markets. In the early 1990s, I saw an advertisement that said a seminar was being held on franchising businesses. I guess this consulting company was a type of precursor to the television show, "Shark Tank." The company looked at different concepts and determined if they thought the concept could be franchised. If they thought a business was a good idea, they would charge a fee to help with the legal work and advertising expenses to get started. I decided it was worth my time to drive to Chicago to tell my story and present my idea about window cleaning. They not so politely said, "NO thank you. It won't work." Rejection is never easy, but I believed this rejection was only one opinion and not everyone's. However, looking back on this experience, it was good they rejected my idea. I really did not have a refined system that was ready for prime time.

In May 1995, my administrative assistant told me she was getting married and moving. My wife, Linda, was working for Hickey College in public relations. I went to Linda and said, "Fish Window Cleaning needs you more than Hickey College. Please come to work for me." We were partners in marriage and managing the mobile home court. Linda had always supported me and helped with some customer billings, but she had not worked full-time in the office. By this time, we had closed our tax and bookkeeping service, so she was open to my job offer. On May 15, 1995, Linda came into the business and things changed forever, and for the better. I didn't know how disorganized things were until Linda showed up.

MANY HATS

On Linda's first day in the business, it was a beautiful spring day, and we were super busy. Cleaners were checking in their completed work orders and getting new work to start the day.

The phone was ringing off the hook with customers wanting to schedule. Linda had always supported me behind the scenes with the window cleaning business, but she did not realize how many moving parts the business had. Linda, like most people, had looked at the business from the outside and thought, "What is the big deal? It's a simple little window cleaning business." But the view is totally different when you are on the inside looking out. By noon, Linda said, "Get me out of here," and we went to lunch. She did not realize the owner of a business has to wear many different hats throughout the day. I will never forget her saying, "I have a whole new respect for what you do, and I never realized what it takes to run the business."

After lunch, Linda returned to the office and started to get things organized. She respected that I should be the person to manage the window cleaners. She said our office roles would be similar to riding a tandem bicycle. Both of us would pedal, but I would hire and train the window cleaners and steer the business. Linda infused a new energy into me and into the office.

LET'S PUT FUN INTO FUNCTION

She began tackling one of the areas that was near and dear to both of us. We needed to improve how we collected money from businesses that did not pay at the time of service. She started reviewing our accounts receivables and an aging report showing if unpaid invoices are thirty days, sixty days, or ninety days old. My previous admin person did an okay job of posting what was due when an invoice was brought back to the office, but she only mailed statements to the customer and did not follow up with a phone call if the payment was not received. Linda understood there was a big difference between posting and collecting and did not hesitate to call customers who were past due on payments. She also mailed invoices and statements pronto after window cleaning jobs were completed. There was no need to wait until the end of the week or the end of the month to send a customer the bill. Being proactive and not reactive is the key to good cash flow. Constant overhead expenses, such as rent and payroll, do not wait for slow-paying customers to mail a check.

Our mantra became:

- Sell it
- Clean it
- Collect it

CONTROL FREAKS

Linda quickly realized I was the bottleneck through which everything had to flow. Without realizing it, I was the control freak in the business. If someone had a question, they would ask me. I basically knew all the jobs, and how to schedule the routes and employees. I knew what equipment was needed, and how to contact vendors. I opened and closed the business each day. I had fallen into the trap of the business owning me.

Linda knew she could not move forward with organizing the office until she could get the information out of my head and on paper. Without saying it, Linda understood the difference between working on the business rather than working in the business. We needed to develop systems that would create efficiencies in order for the business to grow. Another benefit would be to improve our mental health. An activity that consists of shuffling paper around is not the same as productivity.

Business will not grow past the point of someone who thinks they have to control all decisions. The lessons we were learning were foundational. Systems were being developed that would allow us to replicate our business. We may not have known it at the time, but the road was being paved that would eventually lead the way to start offering franchises.

LET'S GET PERSONAL

It was about this time we bought our first PC. QuickBooks was a program developed for the DOS operating system. Linda attended the local community college to learn QuickBooks. We started entering all our customers into this database. This was pivotal in organizing our customers and tracking billing and accounts receivable. We could not schedule our window cleaning jobs in QuickBooks, but a way to do this was on the horizon.

We could not have been more excited when we bought our first fax machine. This allowed us to communicate with customers and vendors much the same way we do now with scanning and email. It was almost magical as we placed an invoice on the fax and hit send, knowing it would arrive in the hands of a customer within a few seconds. As a result, we now had a tool that gave us the ability to shorten the pay cycle for billed jobs, which improved the cash flow tremendously.

I struggled for years with window cleaners leaving the office with work orders and checking in the next day. What happened during their workday was left to chance and their varied abilities to act responsibly. As a side note, not all potential employees are suited to working in an unsupervised environment. Sometimes an individual will need to be hired and given the opportunity to work for a while to really know if they can trust themselves and be trusted. Some employees can really shine, no pun intended, spending all day outside working and meeting people. Good people skills are really important. A customer may remember a friendly smile and a polite thank you as much as the clean windows.

Pagers were almost as transformative for managing employees as the fax machine was for the positive impact it had in office processes. I now was able to page a window cleaner regarding an important change in the schedule. If the window cleaner needed to call the office, he or she would have to find a pay phone or ask a customer to use their landline. I realize some readers are unable to comprehend what living in a world of low-tech was like.

CHAPTER 10

Test the Waters

"Success seems to be connected with action.
Successful people keep moving.
They make mistakes, but they don't quit."

–CONRAD HILTON

In the 1990s, I had a good friend in Tampa, Florida, Al, who was a part-time associate pastor, and he needed a way to supplement his income. Al had worked for me cleaning windows in St. Louis before he left to go to seminary. I thought this would be a good time to find out if folks in Florida wanted clean windows like the people in St. Louis. Sure enough, they did. Using the same techniques in Florida that I used in St. Louis, Al and I went cold-calling. Soon he had a route of businesses that he cleaned on a regular schedule. This was just me helping a friend. This was his business that I helped him get started. He went on to hire one employee, but he kept the business small. Al's love was for the ministry, and he just needed to supplement his income.

In 1994 our oldest son, Matt, was living in Florida and also developed a small window cleaning business while he lived there. This was another confirmation that window cleaning was a valid business that worked in other locations.

STRENGTHEN THE CORE

Matt moved back to St. Louis and rejoined Fish Window Cleaning in June 1995. This was an opportune time to consider expanding the business. Some janitorial companies hire window cleaning companies to do the window cleaning. Janitorial companies do a good job with floors but usually don't have time to train window cleaners. Several janitorial companies were referring window cleaning jobs to me. One day, I received a phone call from the owner of a local janitorial company, and he told me he was going to sell his carpet cleaning business and asked me if I was interested. I said, "Yes." Matt was working full-time and this added service would be a great addition to Fish Window Cleaning. I purchased two vans with mounted carpet cleaning hot water extraction units. Little did I know there is extensive training that goes into cleaning carpets. The carpet cleaning equipment was produced by a company in Indianapolis, Indiana. They offered a week-long training and certification program. Matt and another employee went to Indianapolis to attend the training. A few months later, I took the training as well.

Window cleaning and carpet cleaning seem like two business concepts that should fit hand and glove. We got plenty of carpet cleaning accounts, but our preliminary thoughts did not play out. We anticipated our current commercial window cleaning accounts would also want their carpets cleaned. Statistically, only ten percent of our customers wanted both services. We now chased new carpet-cleaning customers instead of building our core window cleaning business. Commercial carpet cleaning is done at night after the business closes. It didn't take long to realize we had traded a family-friendly, daytime business for working around the clock. One morning Matt came into the office and had been working for twenty-four hours straight. We looked at each other and said, "What have we done? We have lost our focus on developing and growing the window cleaning business." Matt could not continue working to the point of exhaustion, and this was not fair to him or his wife, Tammy. We sold the carpet cleaning business and never looked back. Most business owners get the itch to have add-ons. It is very easy to get distracted, and this experience helped me believe it is better to do one thing well.

I tell franchisees that some of what they are paying for is learning from my mistakes. I have been accused of living in the past or not being a visionary. There may be some truth to this, but there are defunct companies whose walls can be papered with the expansion ideas they tried. Companies cannot be all things to all people. Vision isn't enough. You also need the will to do the boring stuff well and with continuity.

CHAPTER 11:

Time to Rock 'n' Roll

"Your brand is the single most important investment you can make in your business."

–STEVE JOBS

I got over the idea of adding another concept to the window cleaning business, but not over the idea of franchising. I had a passion for pursuing this dream. In 1997, I saw another ad in the paper about how to franchise your business. This was a startup company looking for businesses wanting to expand by offering franchises. I met with them, and they said, "Yes, we can get you started in franchising your business," and they did.

After this company said they could franchise the business, my first question was, "How much will it cost me to start franchising?" They explained the total cost would be about $20,000. At the time, I completely disregarded what a friend had once told me. When someone gives you a price, double it and add at least $10,000: you might be in the ballpark. Believe me, I soon regretted not heeding that advice. That the $20,000 estimate was not on the mark is an understatement.

An arm of the Federal Government, The Federal Trade Commission, regulates all franchises. Law firms and lawyers specialize in drawing up legal documents known as a Franchise Disclosure Document (FDD). Unfortunately, the company I was talking with only knew some basics and were not experts. They drafted our first FDD and franchisor contract, but the legal fees had already greatly surpassed the $20,000 estimate.

COUNT THE COST

When Linda and I decided to plunge into the world of franchising, we committed to self-funding this business venture. I later found out that no one in their right mind tries to start franchising without investment partners. We realized this was the riskiest thing we ever tried to do, and we didn't feel right asking anyone else to take this risk. We knew the ship might go down: If it did, we wanted to be the only two people on board. We were fifty years old, and we borrowed every penny we could get our hands on. I learned that banks won't loan money to an entrepreneur with a big dream. They only loan money if there is collateral to back it. We took out a loan on the mobile home park, Wheel House Manor. We took out a second mortgage on our house. We agreed to live like church mice until we could see the light at the end of the tunnel.

FRANCHISE FOUNDATIONS

We had our first FDD and franchise contract. Now, the clock was ticking. We had to create an operations manual explaining how to run a window-cleaning business and create a curriculum for a two-week training program. We had a good foundation to build on; we had run a successful window-cleaning company for twenty years. As we started learning more about other franchise concepts, we were struck by how unique we were. Some franchise concepts are built on the most recent fad. They will soar in popularity and crash from their heights in a few years. My business philosophy has been that slow, steady growth will endure. We did not want to offer or pursue gimmicky ideas that could hurt potential new franchisees.

A franchise is a turnkey business; if a franchisee has a problem, they need resources and ways to know what to do and how to solve problems, hence the need for an operations manual. It took weeks and months to get our systems down on paper. We committed to the deadline of year-end 1997 to have everything ready. In all my years in different businesses, I had never tackled anything as hard as this. I could show someone how to do jobs, but writing a step-by-step description of what to do in every aspect of the business was daunting. Our first manual was at least a six-inch-thick binder, and we felt we were just scratching the surface on what we thought a new franchisee would need.

BUILDING THE BRAND

We trademarked the name Fish Window Cleaning®, but we wanted a logo designed and trademarked to put on business cards, brochures, and other logoed items. We developed a relationship with a printer we used to print our invoices, business cards, and letterhead. He told us his wife was a design artist, and he suggested we meet with her to create a logo design. She asked us if we wanted a whimsical design or a strong design. Without hesitation, we said a design that represents professionalism and strength. We eventually selected the logo design that we still use today.

Everyone wants to know why we selected the colors red and white. The simple answer is it is Linda's favorite color. However, there is a little more to the story. A large percentage of janitorial and maintenance companies use dark blue uniforms. Uniform companies supply this color in every style and size imaginable.

Fish Window Cleaning is not a janitorial company. Two other St. Louis window cleaning companies were trying out the colors aqua blue and bright yellow. We live in a historic city of baseball fans, the St. Louis Cardinals. When we talked with an apparel supplier, we told them we wanted the same color red as the Cardinals. It works.

The next important items we needed were materials to advertise the good business opportunity that Fish Window Cleaning offered. We were now working with a graphics design company to create marketing brochures to attract new franchisees and window-cleaning brochures for franchisees to use to win over new customers. Working with designers was extremely frustrating for me. I am not a very aesthetically aware person. I took art appreciation in college and loved Rodin's famous sculptor, The Thinker. I can understand that type of art, but beyond that, not so much.

I could write a book on some of the cockamamie ideas designers presented us with. One of my least favorites was a type of Charlie the Tuna cartoon character holding a floor squeegee. That firm left the impression that working with a window cleaning company was beneath them. Another firm offered a more well-thought-out idea, which was a Norman Rockwell theme using his illustration, "The Window Washer," from the *Saturday Evening Post* in 1960. This did not fit either. For one thing, it was a high-rise window cleaner who was pictured. We wanted to alleviate any fear for prospective franchisees that they would be cleaning high-rise buildings, not promote it. This idea left the impression that we were only looking backward and not forward. We did eventually meet with a man from our church who was a retired marketing director for Anheuser-Busch. He made me feel much more comfortable, and he would not charge top dollar. He designed some very nice brochures and other marketing materials that took us through our early years.

DEFERRED GRATIFICATION

Our startup costs were mounting, and we did not have our first franchisee. Our window cleaning business was profitable and was our only source of income. We thought we had counted the cost and the sacrifices needed, but we were naïve in a lot of ways.

In franchising, most, if not all, the upfront money paid by the franchisee goes to franchise consultants, advertising, and training expenses. Many franchise companies make money on royalties, but they also have revenue streams from the sales of branded equipment and other products with the franchise name and logo. This is neither good nor bad, in my opinion, but I always believed I should only make money if the franchisee is making money. I decided to set up our system where any discounts on equipment or products were passed on to the franchisees. Our system was set up to make money at the back end; this means our business makes royalties from a percentage of the production of the franchisees.

SQUEEGEE HEAVEN

In the early spring of 1998, we went to New York, to visit the offices of J. Racenstein & Co., who was my long-time supplier of window cleaning equipment. J. Racenstein was founded in 1909 and is a preeminent distributor of window cleaning supplies na-tionwide. I needed a company large enough to ship to existing and future locations of our new franchisees. I ordered supplies over the phone from Racenstein, but this was my first time visiting their headquarters in downtown Manhattan. It took me a while to find the building. I rode the elevator to the sixth floor, and as

I stepped off, the sign Squeegee Heaven greeted me. I met with Stefan Bright, who was the vice president of sales for J. Racenstein. Stefan is also well known within the industry, and he has held the position of safety director for the International Window Cleaning Association since 1993.

I told him I was in the process of franchising the business and hoped to have all of my new franchisees purchase their equipment from J. Racenstein. Stefan responded exactly like a Midwesterner thought a New Yorker would. His words back to me, "How much mark-up do you want me to add?" I said, "None. I want to pass all savings along to the franchisees." He was surprised but willing to work with me and willing to offer a small discount for new franchisees. He didn't think my franchising idea would go anywhere. As I started to leave, Stefan said, "I am going to give you some advice. Do not sell franchises within the five boroughs of New York. The window cleaners here are what we call legacy cleaners in the trade." I took his advice. A few years later we heard an interesting story from a man who became a Fish Window Cleaning franchisee in Westchester County, New York. As he was researching franchises, he contacted another window cleaning franchise and their salesperson told him he could go into Manhattan. After he talked to our franchise salesperson and was told FISH was not offering franchises in that territory, he was convinced we were a company who had integrity.

Over time, Stefan and I became friends; he would come to our conventions and do safety training and tell his side of the story. He was given a lifetime achievement award at the International Window Cleaning Association Convention in 2020. Linda and I were in the audience, and, in his acceptance speech, he acknowledged me and added he didn't give me a snowball's chance in Hell of being successful back in 1998 when we first met.

Fish Window Cleaning's red logo

Fish Window Cleaning's white
logo with red background

CHAPTER 12:

The Dream Takes Shape

"The way to get started is to quit talking and start doing."

–WALT DISNEY

Before we started to franchise, I had moved on from using index cards. We now had computers with Windows operating systems. Our son, Nathan, had a friend from college who offered to develop a scheduling program using an Access database. We used this database to teach some of our first franchisees how to schedule window cleaning accounts.

Our son, Matt, who was working with us full-time in the window cleaning company, had a real knack with computers and the ability to train future franchisees. Linda and I formed a second corporation, Fish Window Cleaning Services, Inc., as our franchise company. Matt agreed to change positions and come to work for us at what we lovingly call "Big FISH." We realized the size of the window cleaning office located in Des Peres, Missouri, was not going to accommodate our start-up business. For a few months, we set up three desks and phones in our home's basement, while we searched for an appropriate office. I'm not ashamed to admit this. Bill Gates and Steve Jobs started in their garages.

In January 1998, we laid the groundwork to start advertising our franchise. I thought folks would beat a path to our door to invest in this new franchise opportunity. Since we had not done enough due diligence in some areas, we did not realize that everyone in the franchise business would tell prospects not to be the first person to purchase a new franchise concept. The failure rate of new franchise concepts is the same as a new business starting up. Things started slowly, which was a blessing. I did not realize to what extent the operations within a franchise company require different skill sets than running a window cleaning company. Over the years, I have talked to people who have looked at FISH and said they would like to franchise their business. I always ask, "Do you enjoy doing what you are doing?" If they say, "Yes," I explain they may not want to franchise, because franchising is a totally different business.

TEACH A MAN TO FISH

The early days of franchising were very similar to becoming parents. We expanded our family by adding Fish Window Cleaning franchises across the country. We greeted each new franchisee with open arms and wild expectations of their happiness and future success. The reader can probably already anticipate how the story goes. Parenting gets complicated. Franchising got complicated. We made mistakes and franchisees made mistakes. We had sincere, good intentions for wanting our franchisees to be successful. But there were times when we did not have the wisdom to coach some franchisees through difficult times.

If I am being honest, I found myself on an emotional roller coaster when situations weren't going as well as I hoped. But there is not a day I have regretted following my dream. We have the best franchisees I know. I thought I would be teaching others. In some areas of life, I have been a student. I met people from all walks of life, some of whom immigrated to our great country in pursuit of the American Dream. Our company has always wanted to foster a company with a family-friendly business model and develop a culture we call the FISH Family.

THE DISCOVERY PROCESS

The Federal Trade Commission has guidelines on how a franchisor can present the prospective franchisee with information. In 1998, important documents had to be mailed to a prospective franchisee. There was a waiting period of fourteen days before a prospect could sign papers to become a franchisee. This was a good rule, so individuals did not make a decision based on impulsive emotions, but one that was right for them. We wanted a mutually beneficial relationship with new franchisees. Franchisors can also decline to award a franchise if it does not seem to be a good fit. If a person contacted us and expressed a serious interest in opening a Fish Window Cleaning franchise in an available territory, they were invited to visit our office for Discovery Day.

Discovery Days are filled with excitement and anticipation. Prospective franchisees were spending the day with us to check out the business. A big part of Discovery Day is taking time to get acquainted. I have conducted hundreds of Discovery Days, and I have never been bored hearing the stories people share. There is always a certain fear factor when people consider opening a business in which they have no experience. Many times, I would tell the guests, if you are not somewhat nervous, I would be nervous. Most new franchisees were making a commitment to take out a loan on their house or borrow from their 401(k) or from the Small Business Administration. Linda and I could identify with the sobriety of this decision because we had mortgaged everything we owned too.

In 1999, we found space to lease with offices in the front and a warehouse in the back. We were a full-time staff of three: Linda, Matt, me, and an occasional temp or part-time person at the front desk. In 1998 and 1999, we awarded twelve franchises. We are grateful Matt had the support of his wife, Tammy, because we were traveling and working very long hours.

RELATIONSHIPS

As a general rule in franchising, the franchisor cannot make earnings claims outside of the Franchise Disclosure Document. However, an active franchisee can discuss financials with a prospective franchisee who is doing their due diligence. One of the first franchises we awarded was to Don in Cincinnati. Don had been the president of a local bank and was let go. Don and I hit it off at once. Over the years, prospective franchisees would call Don. These validation calls were to find out what having a Fish Window Cleaning franchise was like. Don always took plenty of time to talk with the prospect. Depending on how the conversation went, as a former banker, Don would end the conversation by saying, "You did not ask me an important question. Don't you want to know how much money I am making?" With that question answered, it was possible for them to calculate the potential revenue.

As I have mentioned, I started franchising with no outside investors. Don knew when he came into the business, we were not making enough money from franchising. Don always worried about the fact that I was losing money at that time. He was as happy as I was when we came out of red and into black.

Don was a supportive franchisee in several ways. He told me after his first year in business that we needed to have a small convention to get everyone together. He said, "Mike, I don't care if you roast hot dogs in the parking lot, franchisees need to get together." In July 2000, we had our first "convention." It was a step up from his parking lot idea, but not by much. Stefan, from J. Racenstein in New York, flew in and did window cleaning training and safety courses. The daytime classes were held in our office warehouse with no air conditioning. It was hotter than blazes, and we had a thunderstorm that took out the electricity for most of the afternoon. Fortunately, the power came back on by the time we had our first official Saturday night President's Award Dinner in a nearby hotel ballroom.

This was an important event in more ways than one. It was the beginning of developing relationships in the FISH Family. Franchisees love sharing victories and swapping war stories with fellow franchisees. It was one of many ways we were being established as a real, up-and-coming company.

ACCOUNTANTS AND FINANCIALS

In addition to some of the other legal requirements already mentioned, the Federal Trade Commission requires audited financials for the franchisor for the last three fiscal years before the Franchise Disclosure Document issuance date. This means a franchisor needs a balance sheet for the last two fiscal year-ends and a statement of operations, stockholders' equity, and cash flows for the last three fiscal years. The audit has to be performed by an independent certified public accountant using U.S. GAAS. Also, the financial statements must be prepared in accordance with U.S. GAAP (complete with footnotes) and must compare at least two fiscal years.

PROPRIETARY SOFTWARE

Rob Short, a CPA, was referred to us to do the required audit. Rob was a CPA by trade, and a self-taught computer geek who had a great sense of humor. The calendar had rolled over to 2000 and this was about the time that individuals and businesses were introduced to the World Wide Web. Rob was writing web-based programs, and he tried to convince me to hire him to use his accounting skills and programming ability to develop proprietary software for franchisees. You probably have already caught on that I am not a person who embraces the latest fad. Two things Rob explained to me made sense. The program would simplify the way window cleaning jobs were scheduled, and the franchise owner could look at daily production and bank deposits from anywhere they had access to the Internet. Operating a web-based program was cutting-edge technology, at least for a company our size. We wanted our franchise owners to have some flexibility. Many of them had left the corporate world because they were stuck behind a desk in an unfulfilling job. It was very attractive for our franchisees to have the ability to access reports for their franchise office from a remote location.

Rob went on to develop three versions of our proprietary software. We have grown to the point where we have an outside firm that manages our technology and does updates, and we have two in-house employees who provide technical training and support to our franchisees. Rob and I still laugh over his accounting joke he told me when we first met. When asked "How much is one plus one?" A good accountant will answer: "Whatever you want it to be." Rob took a chance on us and. By that, I mean he was not sure if the young franchise company would produce enough income to pay him.

DANG IT, ANSWER YOUR PHONE

Since Rob was working for us, doing an audit of our books was considered a conflict of interest. We needed another CPA. I am a big believer that it is important for a company to answer the phone during office hours. We looked for an accounting firm close to our office. After calling three or four accounting firms listed in the Yellow Pages who did not answer their phones, we finally got a live voice, Kevin Fine with Fine and Associates. Kevin came to our office later that day. Since we were a startup company in franchising, I know Kevin thought, "I hope they can pay the bills!" Today, we are still with Fine and Associates and remain one of their largest accounts. I am not sure if Kevin appreciates Rob's accountant joke that I now tell as my own, but he does laugh. The reason I include this story about Kevin answering his phone is to emphasize how important it is for a service business to have a live person answer the phone for scheduling and customer support. Live Chat and texting are popular tools today. Potential customers or existing customers want answers, and they want them ASAP.

CAST YOUR LINE

Our training room has a wall displaying the quote: *"Give a man a fish, and you feed him for a day; teach a man to fish and you feed him for a lifetime."*

Look around. Every piece of glass you see will get dirty and will need to be cleaned. Professional window cleaners are in demand. We are proud of the service business we created and believe we can teach others to grow a viable business. Our franchisees can cast their lines every single day and keep reeling in more business.

A basic foundation of growing the business is to provide a timely response. Answer the phone and follow through.

CONSULTANT CONNECTIONS

About a year into franchising, Linda found a company on the Internet, FranNet. They were a well-established franchise consulting firm with offices throughout the United States. Linda got an appointment with Joe whose office was in Indianapolis, Indiana. Joe and I hit it off right from the start. He looked at where I was, what I was doing, and took me under his wing. With his years of experience, he tutored me in a crash course about how franchising works and the benefits of working with consultants. Joe understood that window cleaning does not sound warm and fuzzy. Joe said consultants could help explain to prospects it is not what a business does, but what lifestyle a business can provide.

It is very common for an individual who is laid off or gets the itch to invest in a business to contact a business broker. Franchise consultants are types of brokers who talk to prospects about what type of business might be a good fit. Of course, a prospect must be financially qualified before they move to the next step. Franchise brokers have been essential when it comes to finding prospective franchisees. Franchise brokers receive a fee from the franchisor if a referral decides to become a franchisee. Joe and his fellow FranNet consultants took Fish Window Cleaning into their inventory.

Matt, Linda, and I were invited to a regional meeting in Louisville, Kentucky. Matt and I were wearing suits and ties and Linda was wearing a professional business blazer. We wanted to make the best impression possible. We were introduced to eight consultants seated around the oval conference room table. At this time, we had the best quality, professionally-printed materials we could afford. Inside the glossy, white folder with our embossed logo and the tagline, "A View to Success," was a page with the history of our company and three pages with pictures of our three franchisees and their biographies. One was a bio of a former journalist who was now a franchisee in Tampa, Florida. The second was a bio of a successful businessman from Birmingham, Alabama, who wanted a business he could pass along to his son. The third was Don, the former bank president, from Ohio.

Nothing could have prepared us for what happened next. One of the consultants pushed his chair back, almost toppling it over. He stood up and shouted in disbelief with both a statement and a question, "Don bought a Fish Window Cleaning franchise!!?" We had no knowledge that this FranNet consultant had been working with Don for five months trying to convince him that opening a retail hair cutting franchise would be a good investment. It was as if we could see a lightbulb appear over each head of the consultants. The FranNet consultants in that room realized professional executives might be interested in our franchise business. More importantly, the Lord encouraged Matt, Linda and me in ways words fail me to express. Cincinnati, Ohio's metropolitan population was 1.5 million in 1998. Don was one of that 1.5 million. What are the odds?

The word began to spread among FranNet consultants located nationwide. Even though they heard the story through the grapevine about Don, there were still obstacles the consultants faced on how to introduce this business opportunity to other prospects. People would joke and say, "I don't do windows." FranNet had a residential maid service in their inventory, but for some reason, window cleaning did not have the same appeal. We were the ugly duckling. Prospects would say, "Show me something else."

One of the consultants, who was thinking outside the box, presented Fish Window Cleaning to a prospect by saying, "I have a business opportunity that is Monday through Friday, no nights, no weekends, and no holiday work. You have a crew that does all the work, and you have potential business as far as the eye can see. Are you interested?" Almost immediately the word spread about this effective way for the consultants to talk to prospects. FranNet consultants started sending prospects our way. This was the beginning of an exciting franchise chapter for Fish Window Cleaning.

EMERGING FRANCHISOR

In 2000, Linda and I attended an Emerging Franchisor Conference in Minneapolis, Minnesota. The franchisors who attended were start-ups, but I believe we were the "greenest" of anyone. We soaked up every piece of advice we could take in. We were shocked by the honesty of more mature franchise concept founders. They didn't sugarcoat the challenges of growth, but they also encouraged us to keep going even when times get tough. We were invited to tour the campus of the University of St. Thomas. The Schulze School of Entrepreneurship is ranked among the top 25 undergraduate entrepreneurship programs in the country. This is where I saw the bronze Entrepreneur Sculpture. As I viewed this sculpture, I was very emotional. I had never felt so connected to a piece of art. The sculpture is of a blindfolded man chiseling himself out of a stone. The figure is nude and can be seen from the legs up. His raised right hand holds the hammer with which he is about to strike a blow.

In his rendering of the Entrepreneur Sculpture, Dean Kermit Allison gives a revealing look at the self-made man in the struggle to chisel himself from common stone blindfolded. The entrepreneur must trust his instincts. He has no way of knowing how this will turn out. His face bears the marks of those who would stop him while he is in the most vulnerable stage. His hand is battered from misplaced strokes of the hammer, constant reminders of his own mistakes.

Linda and I stood silently, staring at the sculpture. I told Linda I loved her every day since we met. That day I turned to her and said, "Thank you for not holding me back. Thank you for your support along the way as I have tried to figure things out."

"The Entrepreneur" sculpture by Dean Kermit Allison*

Reproduced with permission from artist.

CHAPTER 13:

Grow the Dream

"The real wealth of a family business is not its profits, but the unity, trust, and shared purpose it fosters."

–UNKNOWN

We returned home to St. Louis and our small franchise office with a determination that, by God's grace, we could keep going. Our 1500-square-foot office had a front lobby, a conference room, two private offices, a training room, and a 1000-square-foot warehouse. Dare I say, we and our guests all shared one bathroom. After two years in this location, we were able to expand to the adjoining office space. Hallelujah! We had a second bathroom. Linda, Matt, and I conducted Discovery Days. If the prospect wanted to join Fish Window Cleaning, and we believed they were a good fit, the required documents were signed. Each Discovery Day guest would leave with a copy of Michael Gerber's book, *The E-Myth*. Gerber says things better than I can. He counters the conception that anyone who is good at doing something will be good at running a business. Our franchisees will need to learn very quickly to let go of some of the ideas they think are better. We don't know everything, but they need to give us a chance to show them why things will work if applied over time.

The new franchisee, then, scheduled their training in our office. After completing the two weeks, we had a graduation celebration.

They would return home on Friday, and the following Monday, Matt, Linda, and eventually Nathan, or I, would travel to the new franchisee's home territory to help them set up their offices and start a sales effort to get new window cleaning customers.

SELLING THE CLEAN

Our sales efforts in all franchisees' territories include cold-calling to potential commercial customers. Some people like to call it doing business introductions. Either way, it requires walking through the front door and talking to someone at the front desk, and either getting permission to write a free estimate or getting a business card with a decision maker's name for an introductory phone call. Historically, this provides the best outcome for growing the customer base. Yes, we encourage franchisees to join their local chambers of commerce, BNI (Business Network International), or the Better Business Bureau. Picture a wheel: The hub is cold-calling, and the spokes are other various ways to develop brand awareness in the community that will ultimately lead to new commercial window cleaning customers.

This is one of my favorite stories about how we got connected with vendors. Remember, our small office had one door with the name Fish Window Cleaning Franchise on the front. A young woman walked in professionally dressed in a suit and heels and introduced herself as the sales representative for Hilton, who was building a hotel about a mile from our location. She wanted to develop the hotel's clientele base around those needing longer stays. It would have been the natural thing for her to walk past our door, but she did not. We sat around our conference room table while she conducted her PowerPoint presentation. She hit the jackpot and so did we. A relationship with this hotel was exactly what we needed to book reservations for our one-night Discovery Day guests and trainees who were staying for two weeks. We were able to secure a hotel with a below market rate, two-bedroom suites, complimentary breakfast, and complimentary manager's dinner for our franchisees.

We love to use examples like this to encourage our franchisees that they may be surprised to discover who is behind the door they walk through. It may be a small office with only a few windows, but they may find a business owner inside who owns investment properties with a massive amount of windows. I can verify that I have had hundreds of experiences where I almost did not heed my own advice to not prejudge a business from the outside, and the person I talked to had multiple locations that needed window cleaning.

BUILDING OUR STAFF

We had to make an investment in more staff. We finally hired an administrative assistant who was a temp, soon thereafter, offering her a permanent position. Fran was fantastic. She was willing to pitch in and do whatever we needed. We hired an in-house franchise development person, Tim. Tim had worked as a window cleaner several years prior. More recently he had been working as a sales representative for Sprint. Tim didn't have any franchise experience, but he understood sales and how to talk to people. In May 2001, we offered our youngest son, Nathan, a position to travel and support new franchisees.

Both of our mothers were in their eighties, Linda's mother, Edna, and my mother, Bertha. My father and Linda's father had both passed. We often wondered what our dads would have thought about our business venture. Our mothers volunteered to help us assemble brochures and mailers. We appreciated any help we could get.

Since Fish Window Cleaning was a start-up franchise, we really had to work hard to avoid failures. Everything we did was to establish our credibility and position us for future growth. Linda, Matt, Nathan and I were the road warriors. We believed the more time we spent in the new franchisees' territories, the more successful they would be. There was a period of more than a year when I never went in my backyard. Linda and I came home, unpacked our suitcases, washed our clothes, repacked, and were back at the airport on Sunday afternoon. The driver of the Parking Spot Shuttle at the St. Louis airport knew us by name.

With all the traveling we did, we still joke about not knowing what city we were in! We found, by traveling around the country, that the cities have many similarities. There were outdoor strip center shopping malls, indoor malls, free standing buildings, chain restaurants, schools, and churches. I would say, "If it's cold, I know I am in the north, and, if I see palm trees, I know I am in the south." I would tell a story about something that happened and Matt or Nathan would say, "Dad, you have the right story, but you are in the wrong city."

I am grateful for the commitment Matt made to come to work for the franchise business at the beginning. Nathan joined the business two years later. Matt and Nathan started to work for me making less money than they could have made working for someone else. In fact, both took a cut in pay to come into the family business, not knowing if it would succeed or fail. The boys took a chance on FISH that it would beat the odds. I am very thankful for their faith.

To say things were lean would be an understatement. All this time the boys never asked for a raise and were super careful with expenses. As we grew, we hired new employees and their starting salary was more than what Matt and Nathan made. Linda was paid minimum wage, so it was legal to issue her a W2 tax form. I would write checks to pay bills, and then, on the outside of the envelope, put a date to mail it. I learned which vendors I could push thirty days to ninety days. I was running up a high credit card debt, which was against my own advice to myself. I have often said a person has not really been in business or under the financial gun until they have laid awake on Wednesday night trying to figure out how to make payroll on Friday. It was about year four when I could see light at the end of the tunnel, and it wasn't an oncoming train.

One of the things our sons decided was thoughtful and respectful. When they walked through the doors of the business, we were Mike and Linda. At the close of business, when we stepped back out into the parking lot, we were Mom and Dad, and it's still true today.

CHAPTER 14:

Gaining Traction

"The Entrepreneurial Model does not start with a picture of the business to be created but of the customer for whom the business is to be created."

–MICHAEL E. GERBER

Fish Window Cleaning was gaining traction. *The St. Louis Business Journal* interviewed us and featured an article about FISH with photos.

This article led to an executive with IBM calling us. He and his wife were planning to move to Boulder, Colorado. They wanted to establish new roots and start a new career. When we arranged an interview with them, we discovered he had previously worked for Farm and Home Savings, but a few years prior to me. This couple had the Fish Window Cleaning franchise in Boulder, Colorado, for twenty-two years before retiring.

More inquiries were coming in regarding our franchise. We hired John to join our staff as another franchise development person in addition to Tim.

FRANCHISE MATCH MAKING

In 2003, we caught the eye of another franchise consulting company, FranChoice, led by Jeff Elgin. Jeff saw the potential in

Fish Window Cleaning and accepted our invitation to visit us in St. Louis and teach us how we could successfully work together. Jeff had eight years of experience as vice-president of Franchise Development with Great Clips before taking the helm as founder and CEO of FranChoice, Inc., an uncommon enterprise that operates as a franchise matchmaker. FranChoice recruits prospective franchisees and helps them find the right fit for their entrepreneurial strengths and financial resources. Jeff taught us how to work with FranChoice consultants and prospective franchisees with a method he called Frick and Frack. Our staff learned how to refine our sales process, and our development team was better able to educate FranChoice consultants to understand the best type of candidates. Fish Window Cleaning had tremendous growth and awarded franchises in new markets all across the country.

FISH's growth over the years has come from organic ways, including people discovering us through news articles, the expansion of social media, and existing franchisees referring candidates to us. Still, the primary driver of new potential franchisees, to this day, is consultant networks.

OFFICE SEARCHES

We had outgrown the office space we were leasing in Chesterfield, Missouri, and the lease was about to expire. The push was on to find a new location. We were not sure if we could borrow the money to purchase a building or if we needed to find a bigger leased space. We found an office building that was for sale and approximately seven thousand square feet in size. We put an offer on this building and waited for the inspection report to come through. When it did come, there were issues, particularly roof repairs or roof replacement. The seller was unwilling to negotiate fixing these things, so we did not follow through with the purchase. This was a blessing, because we were too shortsighted to estimate the space we would need with our future growth and the number of additional employees.

Our son, Matt, stumbled upon a unique building in Manchester, Missouri, for sale. Matt called me and said, "I found a place, the location is great. It has offices and room to expand. It is a racquetball and fitness center." My words were, "You can't be serious." With Matt's persuasion, we looked at the building and made an offer. The fitness company was defunct, and we basically bought it off the courthouse steps. We faced what we call a David versus Goliath experience during this process. Our realtor had written the contract with the required amount for a deposit and our willingness to waive inspections and purchase the building in its current condition. Because this property was in receivership, the sale of the property was overseen by a legal process through a St. Louis County court. We had signed the real estate contract and thought we were good. Then, we got the word. Another potential buyer had popped on the scene with an offer for a cash deal over the asking price.

The court date was set. We didn't know what to expect. Linda, Matt, and I arrived with no legal representation. We prayed and left the decision in God's hands. The opposing party arrived with his high-priced lawyer. The judge asked the lawyer to approach the bench, and the lawyer stated his case and sat down. The judge called my name, and I approached the bench. The judge simply said, "Mr. Merrick, do you intend to honor your signed contract?" I said, "Yes, I do." The gavel went down, and the judge proclaimed, "You are the owner of said property." The opposing party and his lawyer stormed angrily out of the courtroom. My legs felt so weak after witnessing what had just happened, I could hardly walk. Matt, Linda, and I left rejoicing and thanking God.

The building was 20,000 square feet with great potential and some real headaches. We moved in February 2004. We converted the racquetball courts into window cleaning training areas, warehouse areas, and meeting rooms. The fitness center had a daycare section with a private entrance. Within a few months, we moved the Fish Window Cleaning Office, which was still located in Des Peres, into the area where the daycare had been.

Our original St. Louis Fish Window Cleaning office, lovingly referred to as "Little FISH," and our franchise operation, lovingly referred to as "Big FISH" were now housed in the same building. Fish Window Cleaning Services awards franchises, trains, and supports new franchisees. Fish Window Cleaning West County has provided commercial and residential window cleaning since 1978. We don't tell franchisees what a good business model looks like; we show them by example.

MISSION STATEMENT

As businesses grow, people, ideas and goals can fall out of alignment. This happens, especially in family businesses. We were referred to a business coach, Donnie with Salesforce One. Donnie was primarily a sales coach. He helped to create a culture of accountability. We had a few planning sessions with him and one of the topics was the need for a mission statement. To be honest, I never really understood the concept of a mission statement. I had seen them on the walls of various businesses, but I wasn't sure the statements always lined up with the practices.

Donnie assured us that a mission statement was important, and that he could guide us through this process. We scheduled a planning day at an off-site location. Donnie positioned flip charts all around the conference room. He would ask questions, and we would throw out answers. He kept digging deep with hard questions about our company. What was our company really about, and where did we want to go? In a nutshell, did our actions match our talk?

At the conclusion of a very long and somewhat brutal day, Donnie had helped us craft our mission statement:

Fish Window Cleaning® will dominate the market and be "clearly seen" as the best and most respected window cleaning company in the world.

> *We will continue to accomplish this by providing:*
> - *Superior service to our customers*
> - *Unmatched support and partnership with our franchisees*
> - *Personal and professional growth to our employees*

THE BLESSINGS OF A BUDGET

As the franchise business grew, and I traveled more, I needed help. Trish applied for the job as my administrative assistant. Trish was as detailed as Linda. Trish was the first person outside the family who I trusted with the ever-important company checkbook. Releasing control of something like this was not easy for me. Trish was careful to document everything and make sure the bank statement and checkbook register balanced to the penny. Even though she was young enough to be my daughter, she kept the office organized and took care of important responsibilities. Trish worked for us for several years and eventually left to have babies and raise her family.

While Trish took care of paying bills and balancing the checkbook, I still ran the business out of my head. I never had a budget.

Like many people, I believed a budget was a hindrance instead of a help. At this time, I kept track of income and expenditures of the mobile home park, Fish Window Cleaning, and Fish Window Cleaning Services.

Executives need a sounding board. We asked Donnie to come back and help with more coaching sessions. Donnie recommended that the key employees take some personality assessment tests. The personality tests did not measure intelligence or aptitude. Instead, the tests looked at indicators of how you respond to challenges and how you work with others. Companies use various assessment tests to identify strengths and weaknesses. Donnie recommended we all read the book *Good to Great*, which develops the concept of getting the right employees in the right seat on the bus. The hope is to improve the performance of team members and build a positive culture.

During these coaching sessions, Donnie perceived I was under a lot of stress. He knew we operated on a shoestring. He finally asked me point blank. "Mike, let me see your numbers." What he was really asking, "Let me see your budget." I told him I didn't have one on paper, but it was in my head. He said, "Then nothing is going to get done until you produce one." I figured I should take his advice since I was paying Donnie to get us back on track. I spent the next two weeks producing an operating budget. When I completed the budget and had mapped out where we had been to date that year and what the projection was for the rest of the year, including projected revenues and expenditures–the proverbial 800-pound gorilla lifted from my back. I have gone from being a non-believer about budgets to preaching that businesses must have a budget. I am amazed at how many small and large businesses operate without a budget, just like I did.

ONGOING TRAINING

Over the years we have invested in ongoing education for our employees. Some training we offer in-house, and some of us have taken courses at other places. We realize it is important to polish our skills and learn from others. Toastmasters is one course that was highly recommended. Toastmasters is a 100-year-old international organization that has helped people become more confident communicators and leaders. The clubs offer a learn-by-doing program created to help you reach personal and professional goals through better communication. Matt, Linda, Nathan and I attended a local Toastmasters Club one night a week for one year.

We were given homework with assigned topics that we presented in front of the class the following week. The pressure of public speaking was increased when one of the class members pressed a clicker each time the presenter used an "aah." At the conclusion of the presentation, the number of "aah's" was announced to the class. The purpose wasn't to humiliate the presenter but to establish the need to improve. Another, somewhat unnerving segment of the meeting, was the impromptu opening speech. The team leader would select a member in the audience and give that person a topic. Without any preparation, except for the few seconds it took for the person to go to the front of the class, that person had two minutes to speak on the given topic. Some of the outcomes from those experiences were laughable. The year we attended Toastmasters was a great experience.

Linda and I attended the E-Myth Mastery Program in Santa Rosa, California, in the fall of 2010. Michael Gerber did not lead the conference, but we were taught materials he developed that went beyond his book *The E-Myth*. Some of the modules covered included:

- The Emerging E-Myth Leader
- Leading Your Company and Your People to a Higher Place
- E-Myth Management Momentum

We brainstormed with other participants about creating and documenting best practices in an effort to create more cohesive work environments. Some of the simple templates allowed us to visualize ways we could transform the way we work and develop a more efficient, innovative, and creative work environment.

We enjoyed the education we received and the interaction with other participants from Singapore, Australia, and across the United States.

This photo of Matt was featured in the
St. Louis Business Journal, 1998

Mike and Linda pictured in
St. Louis Business Journal feature story about
Fish Window Cleaning, 1998

Our Fish Window Cleaning building
in Manchester, MO, 2004

Mike shows off one of the
Fish Window Cleaning vans

CHAPTER 15:

The Power of Community

"The truth is teamwork is the heart of great achievements."

–JOHN MAXWELL

More than one person asked if I was going to write a book about franchising. It did not take me long to let them know that I had no intention of telling someone how to start franchising. I will leave that vast topic to others who are experts.

However, I am an advocate for the franchise business model. Franchising provides a way for franchisors to expand their business quickly and efficiently into new markets. Franchising helps to transfer know-how and technology between different parts of the world. Franchising provides franchisees the opportunity to be their own boss and grow their own business. The franchisor benefits from having more franchisees, as they can expand their business and reach more customers. Franchising is a win-win situation for both the franchisor and franchisee. It creates jobs and opportunities for people to be successful in business. The International Franchise Association (IFA) provided statistics in February 2024, which indicated that franchising brings a total of 8.9 million employees in the United States and a total output of $894 billion dollars.

Franchise statistics aren't just numbers to me. We all want to be a part of something bigger. "No man is an island" is a phrase that means people are connected to each other and need one another to survive and thrive. The phrase is from John Donne's 1624 work *Devotions Upon Emergent Occasions*. People are social creatures and cannot be truly self-sufficient. They need each other and are better together than apart. Connection is important for the well-being and survival of any individual.

CHAPTER 16:

Love What You Do

"It is amazing what you can accomplish if you do not care who gets the credit."

–HARRY S. TRUMAN

Inspired work is loving what you do. This doesn't mean we will be chuckling all day long. But it is very important to enjoy being in the workplace. A relative shared with me a training concept that the HR department was using at a large hospital where she worked. She told me, "You won't believe it. It is called 'FISH.'" She immediately had my attention, and I straight away bought the book.

The book's premise is based on what was happening with customer service at the Pike Place Fish Market in Seattle, Washington. Pike Place Fish Market is renowned for its exceptional customer service, characterized by a highly energetic and engaging approach focused on creating a fun and memorable experience for customers through playful interactions, enthusiasm, and a genuine desire to "make their day," often referred to as the "Fish! Philosophy."

We enjoy having fun with the name Fish Window Cleaning, and we wanted to know more.

BE PLAYFUL

The book challenges the reader to imagine a workplace where everyone chooses to bring energy, passion, and a positive attitude to the job every day. Imagine an environment in which people truly connect to their work, colleagues, and their customers.

The author, Stephen Lundin, outlines four philosophies in his book *FISH*.

Simple practices that produce amazing results are:
- Be There. Be emotionally present for people.
- Play. Tap into your natural way of being creative, enthusiastic and having fun.
- Make Their Day. Find simple ways to serve or delight people in a meaningful, memorable way.
- Choose Your Attitude.

The philosophy of the book *FISH* really resonates with us. We could think of nothing more relevant to the culture we wanted to create in our office and ways we wanted to coach our franchisees to create a positive work environment in their offices.

We were thrilled when Stephen Lundin accepted our invitation to be our keynote speaker at our 2006 convention.

TEAM CULTURE

A strategy that develops an office culture that respects others and creates a team environment does not happen overnight. When we interviewed applicants, we needed to be open to the idea that our salary range would probably not be in the top tier of what other companies might offer. We looked for potential employees who could be excited about joining an organization that offered opportunities for growth and promotion from within.

I am reluctant to mention any specifics because it sounds like a humble brag. However, as founder and CEO, I chose to invest in my employees rather than lining my own pockets. We introduced a 401(k) that matches contributions. We have group medical coverage, and Fish Window Cleaning pays employee premiums in full. We have generous paid time off and annual salary increases and bonuses. We invest in our employees, and they have made an investment to stay with us for five, ten, and fifteen years plus.

I have reflected many times on my experiences at Farm and Home Savings and the memories I have of the customers patiently waiting in a longer line to talk to a specific teller who they liked. Within our talented staff, we have departments and assigned responsibilities, and they have been cross-trained to fill in for another employee. But I am very grateful for our employees who have the attitude and commitment that goes beyond their job description to step up and go the extra mile to make our organization and franchisees successful.

THE FISH FAMILY

Our franchise business model starts with our Franchise Development Department talking to prospects who are interested in becoming a franchisee with Fish Window Cleaning. Primarily, our prospects are referred to us by franchise consultants. Conversations start on the phone and the next part of the process is what we call Discovery Day. The prospect visits our office in St. Louis and our Fish Window Cleaning West County office to witness what the day-to-day window cleaning operation looks like. During Discovery Day, our guests meet all our employees because they *are* Fish Window Cleaning. If we award a new franchise, contracts will be signed, and systems will be enacted to start pre-training and preparation for the upcoming training week spent in our training center.

Our operations department is responsible for the training and ongoing support of our franchisees. But each and every employee is available to talk with a franchisee to admonish, guide, and encourage. Not every phone conversation is about how to optimize window cleaning routes. Some phone conversations focus on talking about the new grandchild.

Our franchisees are very diverse. They come from many different backgrounds. Individuals choose a franchise for a myriad of reasons. Most of our franchisees have a common goal to experience more independence when it comes to their work environment, but they also like the idea of being a part of a national franchise brand. They enjoy the camaraderie they can experience from talking with fellow franchisees on a Zoom call, at a regional meeting, or at our annual convention.

Our company culture is one that strives to help our franchisees be happy with their decision. I have shared with our employees that I want Happy Franchisees. We use the term "FISH Family," and I really want that to be more than a cliché.

CHAPTER 17:

Franchise Networks

*"Some of the best ideas come when you
are on vacation."*

–ANONYMOUS

We knew connecting with franchise organizations that we could learn from was important. Fish Window Cleaning Services has been a member of the International Franchise Association since 2001. The IFA Code of Ethics established a framework for the implementation of best practices in the franchise relationships of IFA members. Just as franchisees need a place to belong, franchisors do as well. IFA's members believe franchising is a unique form of business relationship. Nowhere else in the world does a business relationship exist that embodies such a significant degree of mutual interdependence.

The IFA has an annual convention that provides a plethora of franchise training. Franchise panels and round tables allow franchise concepts of all sizes to interact in educational settings and mingle in social settings. One of the first things we learned from other franchise companies is the importance of recognizing top-performing franchisees. Top producers received award trophies and discounts to attend their respective conventions. Some awards were more elaborate with vacations or cruises. I wanted to recognize top producers but also wanted a way to reward our franchisees who worked hard but maybe did not fall into a top producer category.

REAPING REWARDS

We appreciate our franchisees and want to encourage them to work hard and play hard. We partnered with travel companies to put together group cruises, allowing franchisees to get better acquainted and relax in a fun environment. We have enjoyed these cruises and will probably continue to do them to celebrate milestone anniversaries. One of the disadvantages of a group cruise, however, is that the ship sails on a specific date at a specific time. Some franchisees or employees are not able to participate.

I liked the idea of investing in a nice vacation property franchisees could reserve for a week to relax and recharge. This allows them to pick a date that best suits their schedule. Franchisees can make the decision to give a week to their manager, to help their employees realize how much they appreciate a job well done.

Our first vacation property was a two-bedroom condo in a vacation resort north of Puerto Vallarta, Mexico. Franchisees enjoyed this property, but travel was not always family-friendly when leaving the country. We sold the Mexico condo in favor of another location. We bought our next vacation property in Orlando, Florida, located 1.5 miles from Disney World. Today, that number has grown to five properties, including a Florida beach condo, a mountain condo in Colorado, a vacation home in Arizona, and a beach condo in Alabama.

Our employees also have the privilege of booking a vacation property. This is just one way we want to show our employees how much we value them. We love receiving pictures from our franchisees as they enjoy vacations at these properties.

CHAPTER 18:

Change is the Only Constant

"A generous person will prosper; whoever refreshes others will be refreshed."

–PROVERBS 11:25

One of the personality tests I took several years ago indicated I am a very strong "S." S stands for steadiness. I like to get up in the morning and follow a routine. I am not very adventurous when it comes to food. I am a meat and potatoes man. When making decisions regarding leading our company, I do not jump on the latest bandwagon. I like to plan and work my plan with some degree of certainty. When the winds of change blow, they certainly slap me in the face but, fortunately, they have not knocked me off my feet.

STORM CLOUDS 2008

Our company was doing well. We had refined our systems, the number of franchises was growing, and franchisees were producing higher numbers all the time. However, a storm was brewing, and the average person did not know any clouds were forming. This is one of the reasons I have found it difficult to work with some business coaches. My experiences with business coaches have been a mixed bag. Usually, the conversation centers around what is your five-year plan or ten-year plan? That is tough to answer. I do believe it is important to plan, but there are times, more frequently than not, that unknowns come so fast and furious from around the corner that good plans fly out the window. Our values and beliefs include putting money aside for a rainy day. These cash reserves, which I refer to as my war chest, are essential when the time comes to fight a crisis.

Fish Window Cleaning Services experienced exponential growth from 2001 through 2007. Then, the recession of 2008 to 2009 arrived. This was the worst economic downturn in the United States since the Great Depression. We invited an outside consultant to come visit us. I had met her through my association with the IFA, and she had years of franchise experience. Companies always risk getting top-heavy with too many employees. I call this payroll creep. We were cautious in this area, but we had more employees than we needed. She came in, spent a few days with us, and evaluated our income and expenses. I did not want to hear what she told me. She said, "You will need to cut fast and cut deep. Sacrificing a few will be better than losing the whole." This was easier said than done, especially since I was on the other side of the desk delivering the message to our operations manager and several other employees. We did not award any franchises for over six months. Employees were willing to take on more responsibilities with the reduced workforce. I am grateful the ship did not sink, and we weathered the storm.

PANDEMIC 2020

The economy recovered, and franchise sales resumed. However, I continued to live below my means and contribute to my war chest. The years between 2010 and 2019 were good, with only a few minor hiccups. Then, in 2020, we all woke up and heard words that were new to most of us. We learned words like "global pandemic" and "social distancing."

I do not want to insult anyone or oversimplify the many ways the pandemic affected all of us. But, from a business point of view, it was devastating. Thankfully, we had our building paid off, and we did not have to lay off any office employees. March is when the busy season for window cleaning really gears up for much of the country. Each state and even municipalities had differing mandates regarding workers and businesses. After a few weeks, our window cleaners across the country were considered essential employees for the most part. However, it's impossible to clean banks, restaurants, and schools that are closed indefinitely. Our overall production declined below the production numbers we had in 2017. The moral of the story is "Save":

- **Save to survive**
- **Save to enjoy**
- **Save to give generously**

CATCH US GIVING

One of the best ways to put storm clouds in the rearview mirror is to find ways to bring some sunshine into the lives of others. It is very popular to share random acts of kindness in all forms. It can be as simple as paying for a cup of coffee for the occupant in the car behind you in the drive-through. We at Fish Window Cleaning locations across the country look for ways to impact customers' days positively. What can brighten someone's day more than clean windows?

- Fish Window Cleaning has provided complimentary cleanings of Ronald McDonald's Houses in various cities.

- Franchisees offer free residential window cleaning for breast cancer survivors across the US during Breast Cancer Awareness Month in October.
- Fish Window Cleaning and individual franchisees support the Semper Fi & America's Fund.
- During our annual conventions, we have organized team-building activities which provide funds for charities such as The Circle of Concern and the Leukemia Foundation.
- The International Franchise Association calls franchise owners from across the nation to participate in a day of Franchising Gives Back to support a variety of charitable causes.
- Fish Window Cleaning supports the St. Jude's Christmas Campaign.
- The Fish Window Cleaning Family Board established a Charitable Giving Fund to support educational institutions, the prevention of human trafficking, Feed My Starving Children, and local and international ministries.

CHAPTER 19:

View from
the Pitcher's Mound

*"Life is like baseball. You're the batter,
and life is the pitcher. As long as you keep
swinging, you're bound to get a hit sooner or
later. You can't hit a homerun every time,
but you can keep it in play."*

–ANONYMOUS

As I put pen to paper, I have loved reminiscing through the events of the past twenty-five years, of franchising in particular. When we have our annual Fish Window Cleaning Conventions, we host our events at different hotels in the St. Louis area. During one night of the event, we choose an off-site location to take our franchisees so they can see something besides the inside of a hotel. St. Louis has some wonderful sights to see. Most out-of-towners have heard we are known for being Cardinal Baseball fans.

In 2011, we reserved five party suites at Busch Stadium. Our convention committee, which included our son, Nathan, convinced someone in the event department at Busch Stadium that the CEO of Fish Window Cleaning should be allowed to throw out the ceremonial first pitch. Remarkably, this person said, "Yes."

I had thrown my share of pitches in the backyard as I played ball with my sons, but I had no official baseball experience. What had my staff gotten me into? Rob, a part of our programming software team, had played some baseball. He stepped up to the plate, no pun intended, and became my coach. He measured off the distance from a pitcher's mound to home plate on a section of our back parking lot. During our lunch hours, Rob and I went outside for some practice.

The view from the Fish Window Cleaning parking lot and the view from the pitcher's mound in Busch Stadium, which seats 46,000 fans, is not the same. It is not even close. You think this is child's play. It is not. It is a grown man's manhood squarely on the line. I practiced, practiced, and practiced. My family was praying for me. I did not want to embarrass my family, and I had approximately 250 franchisees I did not want to let down.

The catcher had a little chat with me, and then it was Go time. No practice throws. One pitch was going to define this moment in time. As I walked to the pitcher's mound, I was wearing my red Fish Window Cleaning shirt. It is no accident our Fish Window Cleaning red is the same as the St. Louis baseball team. We love red. I was hoping red would translate to a red-hot throw. The words, "Don't throw it in the dirt," repeated over in my head like a stuck vinyl record.

I was on the mound. I turned and faced the catcher. I set my position. The longer I waited, the more excruciating it would be. My right arm snapped downward as I released the ball. Wait for it…wait for it… There it was: an undeniable strike right across home plate. The crowd erupted in cheers.

Could I throw a strike again? Maybe. Could I throw enough strikes to win a professional baseball game? No way. Strikes are not really what define us in the game of business. When I started Fish Window Cleaning in 1978, I believed it was an honest service business that could provide a good living for my family. In 1998, when we awarded our first franchises, I made it clear this wasn't a get-rich scheme. If a franchisee was willing to work and follow our systems, they could reap the rewards of a family-friendly business. Starting a service business, even with the backing of a franchisor who has had more than twenty years' experience in the field, will still require hard work and perseverance. The training and support we offer franchisees will shorten their learning curve and help them avoid pitfalls, but nothing will take the place of diligence and keeping their eye on the ball.

HERZOG'S RULES

1. Be on time.

2. Bust your butt.

3. Play smart.

4. Have some laughs while you're at it.

–Whitey Herzog

Mike, Matt, and Nathan enjoy the sights and sounds of the game

Mike chats with Cardinals' catcher in 2011 before throwing out first pitch

Mike winds up for the first pitch at the Cardinals' Busch Stadium

Cardinals' mascot, Fredbird, congratulates Mike on throwing a strike

CHAPTER 20:

Fish Window Cleaning Founded in 1978

"Risk more than others think is safe. Dream more than others think is practical."

–HOWARD SCHULTZ

According to most statistics, only a small percentage of businesses survive fifty years. Estimates suggest only one to five percent of companies reach their 50th anniversary. This information is based on data from the U.S. Bureau of Labor Statistics, which also indicates only a small portion of businesses survive past twenty years.

We do not take it for granted that we are approaching our 50th anniversary. Who could have predicted in 1978, when I handed Mark Stobie the check to purchase his 100 accounts, that we would be cleaning windows nationwide?

PUT A PIN IN IT

In our training room, we have a map of the United States. Each franchise office has a red pen representing their location. Upon completion of training, our franchisees put in a red map pin. This is their way of planting a stake in their corner of the world. We take a picture of each franchisee in front of the map at the conclusion of graduation day, and most franchisees have their map pictures displayed on their website.

We had a new training sign installed in our training room and had the company who made the sign do the installation. Nathan was the person who let the man in and showed him where to hang the sign. I need to mention that over the years I never had contact with Mark Stobie, the man I purchased the 100 window cleaning accounts from in 1978. I had no idea what he had gone on to do. The installer who had finished hanging the sign was putting his ladder away, and he asked Nathan, "Do you know a man named Mike?" Nathan replied, "My dad is Mike Merrick." The man went on to say, "My brother is Mark Stobie, and he sold his window cleaning business to a man named Mike." Nathan answered, "That is my dad." The conversation continued with the sign installer asking what the red pins in the United States map represented. Of course, Nathan was bursting his buttons to tell the story of how Fish Window Cleaning had grown to over 275 franchises. Mark Stobie's brother left our office building in a state of shock. I would love to have been a fly on the wall when he told Mark the news.

Training school map shows FISH locations in the United States

CHAPTER 21

The Captain's Wheel of Success

"Throw off the bowlines. Sail away from the safe harbor. Catch the trade winds in your sails. Explore. Dream. Discover."

–MARK TWAIN

I almost decided against adding a few of my favorite stories from franchisees because we have so many really good ones that I cannot include all of them. Here is a glimpse into the changed lives of a few of our franchisees.

One of our franchisees had been a manager for a chain restaurant that stayed open on Thanksgiving. Chris completed his Fish Window Cleaning training in June. Linda received a phone call from Chris the Friday after Thanksgiving. Chris called our office to express his gratitude. "Linda, this is the first Thanksgiving I have eaten dinner with my family in twelve years. I love this business, and it is truly family friendly." We learned, about a year later, that Chris called a former fellow manager at another location who was cooking about 100 turkeys and told him how much he was enjoying Thanksgiving dinner at home. That former manager and friend is now also a Fish Window Cleaning franchisee.

Another franchisee, Tom, did not know his position as a sales manager for an international company was in jeopardy.

Tom decided to follow his dream of owning his own business without getting a shove out the door. He completed his franchise training in May and, approximately three months later, I received a call. "Mike, today would have been the day." I was not sure what he meant. Tom explained, "Some of my former colleagues let me know that they all received their pink slips by email. The company fired an entire division of employees and used an email notice to do it." Needless to say, Tom was grateful he was now selling and getting new window-cleaning accounts for his own business.

Mike's story is a powerful one that only a few can tell. Perhaps you have been asked what you were doing the morning of September 11, 2001. Most of us were getting the news from our television or a friend who called to tell us to turn on the news. Two commercial planes had flown into the World Trade Center's Twin Towers in downtown Manhattan. Mike was at his desk working for a financial institution on Wall Street. He heard the explosions and went to a Manhattan street to look up and witness the horror. Mike was one of approximately 500,000 people who fled Manhattan over the Brooklyn Bridge in a matter of just hours as dust and debris blanketed the area. This was a life-changing day for many, and Mike decided to pursue finding a franchise that would be his own business and not located in downtown Manhattan.

Tim became a franchisee after working as a clinical psychologist with veterans. This position required a considerable amount of compassion. Tim found he was emotionally spent when he came home to his wife and four children. He had cashed in all of his emotional reserves by the end of his long days counseling others. Tim found the opportunity to open a Fish Window Cleaning in his area. He is grateful, and we are grateful to have him. I talked with his youngest son, Noah, and he asked me questions about business. I told him I liked to read to my two boys when they were young, and they loved the book *The Carrot Seed*, a story of a young boy who planted a carrot seed. His father and mother told him it would not come up, and his older brother told him it definitely would not come up. The little boy pulled the weeds and watered the ground faithfully, but, for days, there was no sign of what was happening below the surface. Until, one day, a big, luscious carrot came up just like the little boy knew it would. I mailed *The Carrot Seed* to Noah, and the next time I saw him, we discussed the business philosophies hidden in a children's book.

The best way to summarize is: Seek advice from people you respect, but not all advice is good. Many well-intended friends would advise an aspiring entrepreneur to be satisfied with a good-paying job and to not take risks.

Our franchisees may not have identical stories to tell, but they all have compelling stories that culminate with the desire for more control in their lives. We call it "The Captain's Wheel of Success." They take advantage of building a business that affords them the opportunity to enjoy more family time and gives them options for expansion, resale, or passing their business along to their children.

CHAPTER 22:

Transitions

"Success is not a destination,
it's a journey."

–ZIG ZIGLAR

As Linda and I matured, we were ready to step back. In 2014, we formed a Family Board of Directors, composed of Matt and Tammy, Nathan and Catherine, and Linda and me. We agreed we wanted to offer the position of president of Fish Window Cleaning Services to Randy Cross. Randy is a franchisee from Grand Rapids, Michigan. I first met Randy in 2002 when he was looking for a business. Like most of our franchisees, he contemplated taking the leap from the secure corporate world into the unknown. Randy and Betsy, his wife, came to our office in St. Louis for "Discovery Day." Randy, like most people, was getting free advice from people who had never been in business. Besides folks telling him he had lost his mind, they told him people in Grand Rapids, Michigan, were too conservative to pay to have their windows cleaned. It took about six months for Randy to make up his mind to become a franchisee in Grand Rapids.

He came to our office for training, and I followed him back to Grand Rapids to help support him. On our first day cold-calling, Randy informed me I was invited over to his house that night to meet his parents and in-laws, and that we had better get at least one window cleaning account that day. The pressure was on.

Cold-calling is always interesting. You do not prejudge any store or location, and you do not walk past or skip any store. As we walked from store to store, it was Randy's turn to go in and ask the person behind the counter if they wanted a free estimate for window cleaning. From the outside, looking into the upholstery store window, the store was a cluttered mess. Randy said, "I am going to skip this one," and I said, "Nope you're going in!" He not only got the account, but they have been a customer for the past twenty-plus years. That store proved that folks in Grand Rapids wanted window cleaning, but it also made the meeting that night with his relatives much more enjoyable. Randy and I have joked about that experience many times.

Randy was a great franchisee who followed the system. Randy believed hiring a good general manager was key to growing his business. His general manager is running the day-to-day operations in Grand Rapids, Michigan, while Randy lives in St. Louis. This location falls within the top five of our overall producers. Randy loves Fish Window Cleaning, and this is just one of the reasons he makes a wonderful president. Randy is a man of faith and has demonstrated in countless ways how he puts others before himself.

When Randy accepted the position as president of Fish Window Cleaning Services in September 2014, I'm not sure the employees really thought I would step away. On Randy's second day, I came to the office in a flannel shirt. The employees realized, then, I was passing the baton. They had never seen me without a Fish Window Cleaning logo shirt on.

The story of Fish Window Cleaning is bigger than one person, me. It is bigger than me and Linda. It is bigger than our sons and daughters-in-law.

Fish Window Cleaning is the story of a service business that continues to develop a unique market niche. The demand for window cleaning is still growing.

The doors of Fish Window Cleaning are wide open, and the welcome mat is always out. We love clean windows, and we believe you will, too.

www.fishwindowcleaning.com

Give a man a fish
and you feed him for a day;
teach a man to fish
and you feed him for a
lifetime.

-Swedish Proverb

Epilogue

"Power coming up!"

–HOWARD HUGHES

In 1983, our family took the trip of a lifetime. I purchased a 24-foot motorhome, and that summer, Linda and our sons, Matt, age nine, and Nathan, age seven, embarked on a 7,000-mile trip out west. We marveled at the mountain peaks in Colorado and rented a Volkswagen vehicle called "The Thing" to drive up Pike's Peak.

We held our breath as I learned to maneuver our RV on narrow, two-lane roads where it was impossible to see what was around the next curve. Our first view of the Grand Canyon was awe-inspiring. We were fascinated by Mesa Verde as we learned the history of the ancient cliff dwellings. We camped mostly in national or state parks, with an occasional stay at a Kampgrounds of America (KOA) campground that had a swimming pool.

We eventually made it to San Diego, California. The deep blue water of the Pacific Ocean did not disappoint. The 2,000-mile drive to reach the coast was worth it. We made our way north to Los Angeles, where we visited relatives and spent a magical day at Disneyland.

One of the tourist attractions I wanted to see was in Long Beach, California. I had read the history of the airplane built by aviator Howard Hughes. Hughes called the aircraft the H-4 Hercules. However, skeptics and naysayers dubbed it the "Spruce Goose." In 1983, at a cost of $25 million, a dome was built to house the Spruce Goose. Tourists could gaze upon the 320-foot wingspan of the behemoth.

In 1942, the U.S. War Department needed to transport war material and personnel to Britain. Allied shipping in the Atlantic Ocean was suffering heavy losses to German U-boats, so a requirement was issued for an aircraft that could cross the Atlantic with a large payload. Wartime priorities meant the aircraft could not be made of strategic materials, such as aluminum. Hughes developed a laminating process called Duramold, and the plane was built using birch wood.

Only one plane was built, and it was never used during the war. Hughes was determined to prove the prototype flying boat could fly. On November 2, 1947, the taxi tests began with Hughes at the controls. His crew included Dave Grant as copilot, two flight engineers, Don Smith and Joe Petrali, sixteen mechanics, and two other flight crew. The H-4 also carried seven invited guests from the press corps and an additional seven industry representatives. In total, thirty-six people were on board.

After picking up speed on the channel facing Cabrillo Beach, California, the Hercules lifted off, remaining airborne for 26 seconds at 70 feet off the water at a speed of 135 miles per hour for about one mile.

Hughes was quoted as saying before a Senate hearing: "The Hercules was a monumental undertaking. It is the largest aircraft ever built. It is over five stories tall with a wingspan longer than a football field. That's more than a city block. I put the sweat of my life into this thing. I have my reputation all rolled up in it."

Individuals find inspiration from a variety of sources. The Spruce Goose was inspirational for me. In 1978, I started Fish Window Cleaning in St. Louis, and in 1983, I already had the

spark of an idea about how to develop the concept of a professional window cleaning company that could grow into multiple
locations. I believed this idea could be big, even Herculean.

I purchased a print of the H-4 and had it framed when I
returned home from our family vacation. This print hung in my
office for thirty-five years and hangs in my home office today.
An employee gave me a model of the Spruce Goose to go along
with the print, which serves as a visual reminder that a dream can
become reality.

Your inspiration may not be a plane made out of birch wood,
but may I encourage you to find someone or something to inspire
you to dream big. I hope the story of Fish Window Cleaning,
which includes the past, present, and future, will inspire you.

Mike holds a model of the famed Spruce Goose, a source of inspiration

Reflections

At times, we all are prone to reflection and reminiscing. Regardless of age, you most likely have heard that time flies the older you get. This is true. Moments vanish and are gone in the blink of an eye. My mother-in-law, who lived to be ninety-five, would say, "Every day is a bonus day."

When Linda and I set out to write a book, our mutual purpose was to provide some insights into business practices and give God the Glory for His blessings on our bonus days. The Providence of God has caused our paths to cross with people from all walks of life in inexplicable ways. We are grateful for the people we have learned from, laughed with, and even those with whom we have disagreed. We continue to pray that we will have teachable spirits.

Some people in the office tease me about things that I say over and over. They call them "Mikeisms." Please indulge me as I share a few.

"You only have 100 percent to work with."

A 100 percent factor seems so obvious. But if you are a budding entrepreneur, there is the temptation to dream your way to profitability. Entrepreneurs must wake up and develop a financial plan. Expenses cannot exceed income.

"It is easier to curb enthusiasm than raise the dead."

Enthusiastic people may make mistakes when they take risks, but enthusiasm and risk taking are required to build a business.

"If it doesn't work on paper; it won't work."

This means you must pay attention to details. Hoping and dreaming cannot overcome a faulty idea. Carpenters use a plumb line to ensure a wall is straight, and a plumb line represents a solid foundation that is essential for the success of a business.

"Give generously."

The Bible teaches, "It is more blessed to give than to receive" in Acts 20:35. Some people believe they will give generously after they make more money. Give now and give more when you can.

"You only go around once, so love what you do."

I am a big believer that it is important to love what you do. Love and enjoy your work and your leisure.

We are thankful for family, friends, and work associates who have encouraged us along the way. We appreciate the many ways our lives have been woven together.

–MIKE AND LINDA MERRICK

Mike and Linda share a laugh

About the Authors

Mike and Linda Merrick

Mike Merrick began his career in the banking industry but decided it was time for a change and pursued the American dream. With a step of faith, he found a promising niche in the service industry, and in January 1978, he founded Fish Window Cleaning® in St. Louis, Missouri.

Linda Merrick was instrumental in working alongside Mike in other business endeavors. Her experience volunteering in several community organizations and working in public relations at a local college prepared her for one of the roles she would play:

event organizer with Fish Window Cleaning. Linda is quick to admit that, at first, she did not see the unlimited potential and demand for this type of cleaning service, which provides professional window cleaning for low-rise commercial buildings and residences. For twenty years, Mike and Linda grew Fish Window Cleaning to the largest window cleaning company in the St. Louis metropolitan area, focusing on repeat, low-rise commercial business. Mike and Linda saw an opportunity to expand beyond St. Louis and, using the franchising model, they began to share the FISH system with others. Fish Window Cleaning soon became a pioneer in the franchise industry and an attractive option for other entrepreneurs looking to join a solid franchise organization. In the first four years of franchising, Linda and Mike trained and opened every new franchise. "We practically moved in with some of our franchisees to spend as much time with them as it took to build a solid customer base," Linda says.

From day one, their vision for FISH was rooted in a commitment to exceptional customer care. As Mike puts it simply, "We show up." Mike and Linda grew FISH's company culture and franchise system on a core set of values. Central to this is a family-friendly business model that promotes work-life balance with no nights, no weekends, and no holidays required. Their deep experience in the business enables them to say, "Fish Window Cleaning is a business you can own without it owning you."

Today, Mike and Linda do not travel for field support trips. Still, Mike is willing to offer support to franchisees, helping them understand their financials and, in particular, the profit and loss statement to maximize their business potential.

Linda and Mike believe it is important to listen to and learn from their franchisees, whom they consider business partners. It is very rewarding when a franchisee says, "Thank you for giving me this opportunity to invest in something I can call my own."

AWARDS

Franchise 500 plaques awarded by Entrepreneur

Mike and Linda receive the Franchise Business Review Top 50 Award

Mike and Linda are honored with the BBB Torch Award

CONVENTION HIGHLIGHTS

Mike and Linda at the Going the Distance Convention

Mike and Linda, Fish Window Cleaning
39th Anniversary

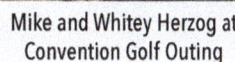

Mike and Linda at Busch Brewery Convention party, 2016

Mike and Whitey Herzog at
Convention Golf Outing

Mike and Randy Cross rock 'n' roll with
Elvis at FISH Convention

1970s anniversary cruise party, 2024

CASUAL OFFICE

Mike sports a squeegee, a tool at the heart of
Fish Window Cleaning's success

Mike and Linda's granddaughter, Eve,
working at Fish, 2018

Mike and Linda's grandson, Sam,
joins FISH, 2023

Mike and Randy Cross brainstorm

Mike, Linda, and Randy prepare for the holidays in 2014

Employees celebrate the expansion of Fish Window Cleaning West County at ribbon cutting ceremony, 2023

Two Fish employees tackle an unusual window cleaning job at the St. Louis Butterfly House

CASUAL

Mike and Linda's grandkids, Sam and Eve, participate
in Manchester Days Parade

Mike and grandson, Sam, enjoy a different
type of "cruising" in Mike's Thunderbird

Mike and Linda enjoy a cruise to reward
top-producing franchisees

Mike and Linda on a vacation cruise

Mike and Linda enjoy some free time on a support trip

Nate and Matt take in a soccer game